The
Astrologer's Guide
Anima Astrologiae;
or
A Guide for Astrologers
Being
The One Hundred and Forty-six
Considerations of the
Famous Astrologer
Guido Bonatus

Translated from the Latin
by Henry Coley,

Together with
The Choicest Aphorisms of the
Seven Segments of
Jerom Cardan of Milan

Edited by William Lilly (1675)
with Notes and A Preface
by Wm. C. Eldon Serjeant,
Fellow of the Theosophical Society

ISBN: 0-86690-555-3

First Printing: 1886

Current Printing: 2005

Published by:
American Federation of Astrologers, Inc.
6535 S. Rural Road
Tempe AZ 85283

Printed in the United States of America

Contents

Editor's Preface

Those whose pursuits have led them to collect works on the Science of Astrology will doubtless recognize in this a work that has long been a desideratum.

To all who have properly studied the various branches of Judicial Astrology, the utility of the Considerations of Bonatus, and the Aphorisms of Cardan, will be manifest after even the most casual perusal. William Lilly, the clever Astrologer of the seventeenth century, specially selected these from a mass of writings at his disposal, for publication at a time when a knowledge of Astrology and a belief in the science were almost general among the educated classes. In a short account of the life of Lilly which appeared in the *Magical and Physiognomical Mirror* for October 1791, it appears that this was the last work published by that eminent Astrologer. The following is a verbatim extract: "His last publication was his *Guide for Astrologers*, translated from the Latin of Guido Bonatus, a good piece."

The lapse of two hundred years and the fate that awaited books of this character in the early part of the nineteenth century have served to scatter and destroy all but a few copies of the edition printed in 1678, and the very existence of this work is at present known only to assiduous students of astrological lore, and to the fortunate possessors of the few copies that remain, which is probably the chief reason why the book has never been reprinted.

Very little seems to be known of the life of Guido Bonatus. Henry Coley, in his "Address to the Reader," herein gives an anecdote illustrating the skill of Bonatus, whose writings undoubtedly prove him to have been an able master of the science which he professed.

Jerome Cardan, author of the Aphorisms contained in the latter portion of this book, was born at Milan on the first of October 1501. He was an illegitimate child, and his mother tried to prevent his being born alive, but without effect. Ultimately, he was brought into the world by means of the Caesarian operation, and when born, his head was already covered with black curly hair.

In the year 1531, he married, though previously deterred by considerations relating to his own physical condition, which he attributed to the evil influences of the planet under which he was born, and always regarded as one of the greatest misfortunes of his life.

He was brought up as a physician, and became a professor of medicine in most of the Italian universities. In the year 1570, he was put into prison; on being released he repaired to Rome, where he attended Pope Gregory XIII as a physician, for which he received a pension until the year 1576, when he died.

Never was a man more remarkable for a strange inconsistency of behavior than Cardan. His life was a series of odd adventures, which he has committed to writing with a simplicity, or rather a freedom, seldom to be met with among the learned; indeed, it seems as if he had written the history of his life for no other purpose than to give the public an amazing instance of the fact that a person may be endowed with great genius, yet at the same time be void of reason.

He makes an ingenuous confession of his good and bad qualities. He seems to have sacrificed every other consideration to a desire of being sincere; and this sincerity being often misplaced, tarnishes his reputation.

Cardan seldom errs when giving an account of his morals and sentiments, yet we must rather incline to dissent from, than to believe, what he relates of himself because it seems almost impossible that nature could have formed a character so capricious and inconsistent as he makes himself out to be.

He paid himself congratulatory compliments on not having a friend in the world, but that in lieu of which he was attended by a Spirit partly emanating from Saturn, and partly from Mercury, who was the constant guide of his actions, and teacher of every duty which he was called upon to perform.

He also stated that he was so irregular in his manner of walking the streets as to induce those who observed him to point at him as a fool. Sometimes he walked very slow, like a man absorbed in profound meditation; then suddenly quickened his steps, and accompanied them with very ridiculous attitudes.

In Bologna his delight was to be drawn about in a mean vehicle with three wheels. The liveliest description that can be given of this singular philosopher is couched in the following quotation from Horace, which in fact Cardan confessed to agree perfectly well with his character:

Nil aequali homini fuit illi; sepe velut qui
Currebat fugiens hostem, persaepe veluit qui
Junonis sacra serret; habebat saepe ducentos,
Saepe decem servos, etc.

Which may be imitated thus:

Where find a semblance of inconstancy?
Now quick of speed, as if from foes he fled,
Now slow he moves, and with a solemn air,
As if great Juno's altar he'd approach;
Now with attendants crowded, now alone, etc.

When nature did not visit him with any pain he would inflict it on himself by biting his lips and pulling his fingers with such violence as sometimes to draw tears from his eyes; and the reason be assigned for so doing was in order to moderate certain impetuous sallies of the mind whose violence was far more insupportable to him than pain itself; and that the sure consequences of such severe practice procured his better enjoyment of the pleasures of health.

He writes that in his greatest tortures of soul, he used to whip his legs with rods and bite his left arm; that it was a great relief to him to weep, but that very often he could not; that nothing gave him more pleasure than to talk of things which made the whole company uneasy; that he spoke on all subjects, whether seasonably or not; and that he was fond of all games of chance as to spend whole days in playing at them to the great prejudice of his family and reputation, for he even staked his furniture and his wife's jewels.

Cardan scrupled not to own that he was revengeful, envious, treacherous, a dealer in the black art, a backbiter, a calumniator, and unreservedly addicted to all the foul and detestable excesses that can be imagined; yet notwithstanding so humiliating a declaration, there never was, perhaps, a man more vain, or one that with less ceremony expressed the high opinion he had of himself. He writes thus:

"I have been admired by many nations; an almost infinite number of panegyrics in prose and verse have been composed to celebrate my fame. I was born to release the world from the manifold errors under which it groaned. What I have found out could not be discovered either by my predecessors, or my contemporaries; and that is the reason why those authors who write anything worthy of being remembered blush not to own that they are indebted to me for it. have composed a book on the dialectic art in which there is neither a superfluous letter, nor one deficient. I finished it in seven days, which seems a prodigy. Yet where is there a person to be found that can boast of his having become master of its doctrine in a year? And he that shall have comprehended it in that time must appear to have been instructed by a familiar Demon."

When we consider the transcendent qualities of Cardan's mind, we cannot deny his having cultivated it with every species of knowledge, and having made a greater progress in philosophy, in medicine, in astronomy, in mathematics, etc., than the majority of his contemporaries, who had applied their study but to one of those sciences.

Scaliger, who wrote with much warmth against Cardan, was candid enough to own that he was endowed with a very comprehensive, penetrating, and incomparable mind.

Cardan has been accused of impiety, and even atheism, because in his work, *De Subtilitate*, he quotes some principles of different religions, with the arguments upon which they were founded. He proposes the reasons offered by the Pagans, by Jews, by Mahomedans, and by the Christians, but these of the last in the weakest light. Nevertheless, in reading one of his works, *De Vita Propria*, we find more characteristic marks of a credulous man than a free-thinker.

It is true that he owns he was not a devotee, *parum pius*, but he at the same time declares that although naturally vindictive, he often let slip the opportunity of satisfying his resentment. Let such a neglect, then, be ascribed to his veneration of the Deity, "*Dei ob venerationem.*"

He writes, "There is no form of worship more pleasing to Deity than that of obeying the law, against the strongest impulsion of our natures to transgress against it." He proudly boasted of having refused a considerable sum of money offered to him by the King of England, on condition that he would give him those titles which the Pope had taken from him. It would be difficult to find in any work proofs of more solidity and good sense than in the reflections made by him in the twenty-second chapter of the above-mentioned book, where he unfolds his ideas of religion. The reason which he assigns for his love of solitude, instead of making him liable to the charge of impiety, ought rather to free him from the same. "When I am alone," he writes, "I am then, more than at any other time, in company with those I love—the Deity, and my good Angel."

Cardan had many irregular faculties that were more bold than judicious, and was fonder of a redundancy than a choice of materials to work upon. The same capriciousness observable in his moral conduct is to be remarked in the composition of his works.

There are a number of his treatises in which the reader is stopped almost every moment by the obscurity of the text, or the digressions from the subject in point.

In his arithmetical works there are several discourses on the motions of the planets, on the Creation, and on the tower of Babel.

In his dialectic work, he gives his opinions on historians and the writers of epistles. The only apology which he makes for the frequency of his digressions is that they are purposely done for the sooner filling up the sheet, his bargain with the bookseller being at so much per sheet, and that he worked as much for his daily support as for the acquisition of glory.

Cardan was instrumental in reviving the sacred philosophy of the Cabala, and the Cabalists. The Aphorisms of his Seven Segments, contained in this book, are of great value to Astrologers.

For the information of those who might peruse this work, and who know little or nothing of the science on which it treats, we may mention that Astrology is held to be one of the most ancient of all sciences. Josephus[1] writes that Adam, Seth, Enos, and most of the Patriarchs were great Astrologers, and after them Abraham, who taught both the Chaldeans and Egyptians. The same historian states that he has seen the remains of the two pillars of stone upon which Seth, foreseeing the flood, engraved the rudiments of the science.

This book does not profess to be an elementary work; it is intended for the use of students somewhat advanced in Astrology. To persons desirous of thoroughly learning this branch of occult philosophy, we recommend the works of the following writers: On Genethliacal Astrology—Ptolemy[2], Placidus[3], Partridge[4], Wilson[5], Oxley[6], Morrison (Zadkiel)[7], and Pearce[8]. On Mundane Astrology, the Doctrine of Elections, Decumbitures, etc.—Ptolemy[2], Ramesey[9], and Saunders[10]. On Horary Astrology—Lilly[11] and Zadkiel[12]. On

Astro-Meteorology—Goad[13]. The works of Doriat[14], Heydon[15], Ball[19], Penseyre[17], Coley[18], Eland[19], Salnon20, Worsdale[21], Simmonite[22], Raphael[23], Shemaya[24], and Zuriel[25], are worthy of the student's perusal, and much useful information can be gleaned therefrom. The works of Ramesey and Partridge are rare and priceless. In fact, most of the older works quoted are now very scarce. They can all be seen and read at the British Museum, but are to be met with in very few private libraries.

The science of the stars has of late years fallen into disrepute, chiefly owing to impostors, but also to zealous persons endeavoring to practice an art in which they have not been sufficiently well read to give correct judgments; not a little, however, does it owe its present position to the erroneous publications on the subject, which from time to time have been palmed off on the unsuspecting and anxious students as works of use and value.

The desire and belief of the present editor is that the republication of a few of the more philosophical works relating to this science may win for it some degree of recognition from the large and increasing body of students of the Occult Sciences; these views are shared by the publisher, who has ventured upon the unusual course of issuing, in this skeptical age, a work professing seriously to deal with the Science of the Stars.

Near Bodmin, Cornwall
16th April, 1885

References

[1] Joseph. Antiq., B.I., ch. 4-8, etc.

[2] *Ptolemy's Tetrabiblos*; translated by Ashmand, 8 vo. London, 1822.

[3] *Primum Mobile*, Placidus de Titus; translated by John Cooper, 8 vo., N.D.

[4] *An Astrological Vade-Mecum for Students in Astrology*; by John Partridge, 12 mo., London, 1678.

Opus Reformatum; by John Partridge, 4 to., London, 1698.

Defectio Geniturarum; by John Partridge, 4 to., London, 1697.

[5] *A Complete Dictionary of Astrology*; by John Wilson, 8 vo.

[6] *The Gem of the Astral Sciences*; by Thomas Oxley, 8 vo.

[7] *The Grammar of Astrology*; by Zadkiel, 12 no., London, 1849.

The Handbook of Astrology; by Zadkiel, Vol. II (Nativities), small 8 vo., London, 1864.

Zadkiel's *Legacy, Essay on Astrology, Nativity of H.R.H. the Prince of Wales*, etc.; 8 vo., London, 1842.

[8] *The Text-Book of Astrology*, Vol. 1, Genethliacal; by Alfred J. Pearce, 8vo., London, 1879.

[9] *Astrology Restored*; by William Ramesey, folio, London, 1654.

[10] *The Astrological Judgment and Practice of Physic*; by Richard Saunders, 8 vo., London, 1677.

[11] *Christian Astrology*; by William Lilly, 4 to., London, 1647.

An Introduction to Astrology; by William Lilly, with Notes and Emendations by Zadkiel, 8 vo., London, 1835.

This work, together with Zadkiel's *Grammar of Astrology*, has been reprinted, bound together in one volume, and published in the "Bohn" series.

[12] *The Handbook of Astrology*, Vol. 1 (Horary), by Zadkiel, small 8 vo., London, 1863.

[13] *Astro-Meteorologica*, etc.; by J. Goad, folio, London, 1685.

[14] *A Brief and Easy Introduction to Astrology*; by Claudius Dariot, 1598.

Dariotus Redivivus; 4 to., London, 1653.

[15] *An Astrological Discourse*; by Sir Christopher Heydon, 12 vo., London, 1650.

[16] *Astrology Improved*; by Richard Ball, 12 mo., 1723.

[17] *A New Guide to Astrology*; by Samuel Penseyre, 12 vo., 1726.

[18] *Clavis Astrologiae Elimata*; by Henry Coley, 8 vo., London, 1676.

[19] *Eland's Tutor to Astrology*; by George Parker, 18 vo., 1704.

[20] *Horae Mathematicae seu Urania*; by William Salmon, 8 vo., 1679.

[21] *Genethliacal Astrology*; by John Worsdale, 8 vo., Newark, 1798.

Celestial Philosophy; by John Worsdale, 8 vo.

[22] *The Arcana of Astral Philosophy*; by W. J. Simmonite, 8 vo., 1847.

The Astro Philosopher and Meteorologist; by W. J. Simmonite, 9 vo., about 1851.

The Prognostic Astronomer (Horary Astrology); by W. J. Simmonite, 12 vo., Leeds, 1852.

[23] *A Manual of Astrology*; by Raphael, 8 vo., London, 1837.

[24] *The Star*; by Ebn Shemaya, 8 vo., 1839.

[25] *Lectures on the Science of Celestial Philosophy*; by Zuriel, 8 vo., 1835.

Editor's Preface
to the 1953 Edition

Because the present Editor and Publisher heartily endorse the motives which prompted the 1886 republication of this work, which has long since been out of print and unavailable to most twentieth century students of astrology, this edition is being made available.

Strangely enough, or is there a cosmic cause that is the *Primum Mobile*, he is prompted to commence preparation of this edition on another April 16, sixty-seven years later.

While the environment of civilization, in the light of which all astrological delineation must be made, has changed radically since Guido Bonatus and Jerome Cardan first set these aphorisms down, the basic material is so important and of such value to students of astrology today that it is felt that it must be made available to then. It is with this sole purpose that it is so dedicated.

Washington, D.C
16th April, 1953

Address by William Lilly to the Ingenious Lovers of Art

We had formerly some thoughts of revising our *Introduction to Astrology*, now out of print, and to have enriched it for another edition with the choicest aphorisms, both from the writings of the ancients and our own many years' experience, but the laboriousness of that work, considering our age and many infirmities of body, with the discouragements we have already met with from some ungrateful persons[1], caused us lay aside (at least for the present) those intentions.

Yet that we might not be wholly wanting to promote anything that might tend to the advancement of Art and gratification of its painful[2] students, and knowing how necessary the ensuing Considerations of Guido Bonatus and Aphorisms adjoined, are to be known and regarded, which many of our ingenious countrymen could not do, for that they have hitherto remained in the Latin tongue with the rest of the works of those authors in large volumes, difficult to be got at and too chargeable for many to buy, we therefore recommend them to a friend[3] to be translated by themselves, which he has judiciously performed in plain significant language, so that we judge the work may deserve the title *Anima Astrologiae* which we have given it, comprehending the marrow and substance of Astrology, and much excellent matter

---

[1] Allusion is here evidently made to John Gadbury, the Astrologer, and some of his pupils, with whom Lilly had been at variance.

[2] Laborious.

[3] Henry Coley, one of his pupils, and latterly, his amanuensis.

necessary to be observed by all honest students that practice Art to discover truth and not to vapor with[4].

We doubt not but the legitimate sons and well-wishers of Urania will find considerable advantages from hence, directing them to a certainty in giving judgments upon all occasions, and they will for this publication have cause to thank their old friend.

William Lilly
Walton-upon-Thames
2d August, 1675

---

[4] This is probably a sly hit at John Gadbury, with whose judgments of astrological figures and remarks thereon, Lilly found fault; as indeed at a later period did Doctor John Partridge the Astrologer, who wrote a work (*Opus Reformatum*; London, 1693) exposing and rectifying the errors of one of Gadbury's works (*A Collection of 150 Nativities*; London, 1658). It is a significant fact that Dr. Partridge, who was one of the most truthful of Genethliacal Astrologers that ever lived, quotes Bonatus in his *Opus Refomatum*, thereby showing his esteem for the Considerations of our Author.

𝕳enry 𝕮oley's 𝕬ddress to the 𝕽eader

Thou art here presented with two choice pieces of Art in our mother tongue; the first, the Considerations of Guido Bonatus, a person no less happy in the practice than skillful in the theory of Astrology of which I will here give thee one instance as it is recorded by that eminent Historian Fulgusos, L. 8, c. 11. That Guido Earl of Mount-Serrant being besieged in that city, our Author Bonatus sent him word that if such a day and hour he would make a sally on the enemies' camp, be should give them an absolute defeat, and force them to raise their siege and quit the place, but should himself receive a dangerous (but not mortal) wound in the thigh. The Earl took his council, made his sally on the day appointed, providing himself of all things necessary in case of a wound, and according to the prediction, though vastly inferior in numbers, obtained a most signal and entire victory, but following the pursuit was wounded in the place foretold, of which in short time he recovered.[1]

The second consists of the choicest Aphorisms of Cardanus, a man famous to the learned world, and of whom the judicious and severe Scaliger (though an adversary) in the preface to the book he wrote against him, gives a most respective and applauding character. These Aphorisms (by which is meant short comprehensive and approved rules of Art) were in the original delivered promiscuously, but I for better method have taken the pains here to marshal them un-

---

[1] Raphael quotes this in his work, *A Manual cf Astrology* (London, 1834).

der their distinct and proper titles, and that I might not unnecessarily charge the reader, have omitted such as seemed trivial or superfluous; this much I thought fit to premise, and have only more to add, that by reason of my absence some faults have escaped the press, besides those which myself may be chargeable with in the translation; the Reader will show his judgment in distinguishing, and his good nature in pardoning them. Vale.

H. C.

Proem

Amongst those things that appertain to giving judgment in questions of Astrology, there are six to be chiefly considered: 1st, Nations, and their particular kinds. 2d, Families, and the constitutions and ordinations of Families and Houses. 3d, Rich and potent persons, Dispositions and Affairs. 4th, Regard is to be had to the Individuals of human kind. 5th, Elections or times proper for the beginning of any Work or Enterprise. 6th, Questions as well universal as particular, pertinent and fit to be demanded.

But first of all there are some things necessary to be premised: As to the fit manner of propounding a question, and diverse other points to be observed in giving judgment. Or which sort of considerations we shall reckon up no fewer than One Hundred Forty and Six, which though 'tis impossible they should happen or be observed altogether; yet they all deserve to be known, and without them an Astrologer shall never be able to give true and perfect judgment. But before we treat distinctly of them it will be convenient to say a little of the right way or manner how a question shall be proposed; for to judge of things to come is no easy task, nor indeed can it always be exactly performed; but we may come near the truth, and differ from it only in some small time or circumstances; which difficulty should not at all discourage us from studying and endeavoring to obtain as great a knowledge therein as Human minds are capable of; for since inferiors are governed by superiors (as all agree), and that the nature and disposition of such superiors may be known by their motions, which are now exactly found out by the learned in Astronomy; we may thence undoubtedly arrive at an ability of judging things to come: That is, declare what will happen by or from such their motions, and by consequence truly foretell future accidents; for this art has its peculiar rules and Aphorisms and its end is judgment, which takes off their objection who say that Astrology is nothing worth; for it would not be an Art unless it had its proper precepts; but that it is an Art, we have sufficiently proved elsewhere, and the same is generally acknowledged; and its end is to give judgment as aforesaid, which are of accidents imprinted on inferiors by the motions of the superior bodies, and their qualities and effects in or upon the same.

The Considerations
of Guido Bonatus

1. THE 1ST is to observe what it is that moves a person to propose or ask a question of an Astrologer; where we must take notice of three motions; the First, at the mind, when a man is stirred up in his thoughts and hath an intent to enquire; a Second, of the superior and celestial bodies, so that they at that time imprint on the thing inquired after, what shall become of it; the Third, of the free will which disposes him to the very act of enquiring, for although the mind be moved to inquire, 'tis not enough unless the superior bodies sympathize therewith, nor is such notion of the stars enough unless by the election of his will the person does actually enquire.

2. THE 2D consideration is (what we hinted at before) the method or manner everyone ought to observe that inquires of an Astrologer; which is, that when he intends to take an artist's judgment of things past, present, or to come, he should, first, with a devout spirit, pray unto the Lord, from when proceeds the success of every lawful enterprise, that he would

grant him the knowledge of these things of the truth of which he would be resolved; and then let him apply himself to the astrologer with a serious intent of being satisfied in some certain and particular doubt, and this not on trifling occasions, or light sudden emotions, much less on matters base or unlawful, as many ignorant people used to do; but in matters of honest importance, and such as have possessed and disturbed his mind for the space of a day and night or longer; unless in sudden accidents which admit not of delay.

Note by Lilly—"Those that take this sober course, shall find the truth in what they enquire after; but whosoever do otherwise, deceive both themselves and the artist; for a foolish Querent may cause a wise Respondent to err, which brings a scandal upon Art amongst inconsiderate people, whereas the Astrologer is not blameable, but the ignorant silly Querent."

3. THE 3D is to consider how many ways Planets operate upon Inferior Bodies according to the diverse Qualities of their motions; there being Sixteen different ways of such their operations and effects in all things that are either wholly or in part perfected or destroyed.

4. THE 4TH is to consider particularly these several sixteen ways, and what are the assisting causes that help forward things to perfection, and what there are that destroy things after they are perfected. Now of these the first is Protection, or an advance of or in, things, which the philosophers call "Alchecohol." 2. Detriment, which they call "Aliber." 3. Conjunction or Reversion, which they call "Alitifall." 4. Separation, which they call "Alnichirat." 5. Translation of light, which they call "Annecad." 6. Collection, which they call "Algemei." 7. Prohibition, which they call "Almana." 8. Re-

ception, called "Alcobol." 9. Being void of course, called "Gastalcobal." 10. Permission, called "Galealocir." 11. The restoring or giving of virtue or disposition, called "Alteat." 12. The withdrawing of virtue, called "Dalpha Alchoa." 13. The withdrawer or driver away of disposition, called "Daffaredbit." 14. Fortitude, "Alcoevah." 15. Debility, "Adirof." 16. The state of the Moon called "Gnaymel," or the Moon ill-affected, which the ancients generally held to be of ill signification.

5. THE 5TH is to consider, how many ways the Moon comes to be so ill-affected, which are generally reckoned to be Ten, but in my opinion Seven more may be added, whereby hindrances and damage happen in all Questions, Nativities, Elections, and actions whatsoever; the First is, where the Moon is combust, that is to say under the Sun's beams, which is counted from 15 degrees of the body of the Sun as she applies to him to 12 degrees distance from him as she is separating from him; and the impediment is greater when she is going to the Sun than when she is going from him; because as she goes off, when she is got five degrees distant, she is said to be escaped, though not wholly freed. As when a fever hath left a man, he is said to be recovered, although he be weak and faint, because he is secure now that he shall obtain his health again. The 2d is when she is in the degrees of her descensions, that is in the 3d degree of Scorpio, or in any part of Scorpio or Capricorn or joined with any Planet that is in her or its own descensions, as if she be joined with the Sun, who is in Scorpio or Capricorn or in his proper descension, viz., in Aquary or Libra, viz., in its 19th degree or in any part of Libra; or should be joined with Mars, and he be in Libra or Taurus, or in the 28th degree, or in any part of Cancer; and so with any other Planet or Planets respectively. The 3d is when

3

she is posited in any of the combust degrees, of which the worst are those 12 degrees which are before the degree which is directly opposite to the degree in which the Sun is, wherever she shall happen to be. The 4th is when she is in conjunction, opposition, or square to either of the Infortunes, Saturn or Mars, without a perfect reception; for with one it hinders but little, but in all other places 'tis a grand impediment, both in the said aspect and also in corporal conjunction save only where the Infortune shall have two of his smaller dignities, as with Saturn in the 4 last degrees of Aries or Gemini, in each of which he has a Term and a Triplicity; or with Mars in the last 10 degrees of Pisces, where he has a Pace and a Triplicity; and so in any other sign or place. The 5th is when she is with the Dragon's Head or with the Dragon's Tail, that is, within twelve degrees of either of them, because that is the place where she is eclipsed. The 6th is when she is in Gemini, which is the twelfth from her own House. The 7th is when she is in the end of signs, which are all Terms of the Infortunes, except the last 6 degrees of Leo, which belong to Jupiter; but in the first eight she is weakened because they are the Terms of Saturn. If it be objected by the sane reason she must be impedited likewise in the first 6 degrees of Cancer, since they are Terms of Mars, I answer no, because Cancer is her own House and greatest Fortitude. The 8th is when she is in the VIth, VIIIth, IXth, or XIIth Houses (not in reception with the Ascendant), or joined to any planet that is in any of them or posited in the Third House, because it is cadent from angles; yet because the same is said to be her joy (or that she delights therein), she is not afflicted there so much as in other Cadent Houses. The 9th is when she is between the 15th degree of Libra and the 5th degree of Scorpio, which 30 degrees are called the Combust Way. The 10th when she is void of course, that is, not joined to any planet by body or aspect, or in that condition when they call her Feral or Desart, that is, in a place where she has not any dignity. The 11th when she is slow of course, because then she may be compared to a Planet Retrograde. The 12th when she is in want of light, so that no part or very little of her is seen, which happens about the end of the lunar month. The 13th when she is besieged by the two Infortunes impediting her. The 14th if she be in Azimene degrees. The 15th if in Pitted degrees. The 16th if in Smoky degrees. The 17th and last is when she is posited in those degrees which are called dark. To know and distinguish all which you have Tables commonly in most Books of Astrology.

6. THE 6TH consideration is to regard another manner whereby planets are debilitated or weakened and afflicted, not much different from the former, which comes to pass Ten ways. The 1st, when a planet is Cadent from Angles or from the Ascendant, so that he does not behold the same. The 2d, when a Planet is retrograde. The 3d, if they be combust, that is, within 15 degrees before or after the Sun; the lower Planets are more debilitated, being behind the Sun, and the less before him, when they are direct; but when retrograde the contrary. 4. When any of them is in Opposition, Corporal Conjunction, or Square of either or both the Infortunes without Reception. 5. When they are besieged by the Infortunes, so as to separate from one and be joined to another, without perfect reception of House, Exaltation, or two of the smaller Dignities, which are Term, Triplicity and Face. 6. When a Planet is joined to another in his Declension or Fall, that is, in Opposition to its own House or Exaltation. 7. When it is joined to a Planet Cadent from the Ascendant, or separates from a Planet that did receive him, and is joined to another that doth not. 8. When a Planet is Peregrine, that is, in a place

where he hath not any Dignity; or being one of the Superiors is followed by the Sun, or being of the Inferiors when it follows the Sun. 9. When a Planet is with the Head or Tail of the Dragon, without Latitude. 10. When a planet weakens itself, that is, when it is in the Seventh House from its own, Feral, or not in Reception. These are the impediments of the Planets that cause Hindrances, delays, and mischiefs in Nativities, Questions, Elections, etc.; all which thou oughtest to be well acquainted with. There are some more that seem necessary to be known, but to avoid tediousness and confusion I shall at present omit them.

7. THE 7TH consideration is to beware of those cases wherein the Astrologer is subject to err and mistake; of which the learned have named four: 1. When the Querent is so silly that he knows not how to ask, nor what he would have. 2. When the time for which the figure is erected is mistaken. 3. When the Artist knows not whether the Sun be gone oft the line of the Mid-Heaven, or still upon it, or be behind or before it. 4. When the Fortunes and Infortunes shall be of equal strength; at which time thou therefore oughtest not to receive any Question. But, in my opinion, there may well be added yet three ways more, wherein the Astrologer will be subject to err: 1. When the Querent comes only to try him, or put a trick upon him, as many do, saying, "Let us go to such an Astrologer, and ask him such a thing, and see if he can tell us the truth or not." Just as the Jews propounded questions to our Lord Jesus Christ, not so much to be resolved, as to tempt and ensnare Him. 2. Wherein the Artist will be liable to err, is when the Querent does not ask out of a serious or settled intention, as some do when they meet an Astrologer by chance or go to him on other business; on a sudden they think cf something, and so ask, as it were by-the-bye; wherein 'tis a

thousand to one but mistakes happen. But thou mayest be ready to say, "How shall I know whether the Querent come out of a solid intention, or only to try me?" To which I answer that it seems a very abstruse and difficult point, perfectly to find out; but this I have often experienced and found true, viz., I observed the hour of the Question, and if the Ascendant then happened very near the end of one sign and beginning of another, so that it seemed as between both, I said they did not ask seriously, or that they came to try me; and I have had many that have thereupon confessed what I said to be true, and began to think that I knew more than before they believed. For in such cases I used to say, "Pray, friend, do not trouble me unless you ask seriously, for I suspect that you would put a trick upon me, by not proposing this Question as you ought; however, if you will give me trouble for your pleasure, be pleased to give me likewise, satisfaction for my pains"; and immediately, if there were any deceit intended, away they went. Another, viz., a third way whereby an Astrologer may err, is when the Lord of the Ascendant and the Lord of the Hour are not the same, nor of the same Triplicity, or be not of the same Complexion with the Ascendant; for then the Question is not Radical, as I have frequently found by experience. And this I have recited, that thou mayest know for what persons thou shouldest undertake to give judgment; for as one says, "The issue of the thing is according to the solicitude of the Querent, and as he comes in necessity, as sad, thoughtful, and hoping, that thou art able and knowest how to satisfy him the truth of the matter; and in such cases thou mayest securely venture upon the question."

8. THE 8TH consideration is to mind how many of the aforesaid manners or points necessary to be used and heeded in giving Judgments thou hast to consider; and they are

Thirty, that is to say, sixteen impediments of the Moon, ten of the other Planets; as hath been said; and besides all those the Planets' several joys, which are four. Of which the first is the House which each Planet does delight in, as Mercury in the Ascendant, the Moon in the third, Venus in the fifth, Mars in the sixth, the Sun in the ninth, Jupiter in the eleventh, Saturn in the twelfth. The second is, when a Planet is in a sign he delights in, as Saturn in Aquarius, Jupiter in Sagittary, Mars in Scorpio, Sol in Leo, Venus in Taurus, Mercury in Virgo, and the Moon in Cancer. The third is when Diurnal Planets, as Saturn, Jupiter, Sol, and Mercury, are in Diurnal Houses in the East and Oriental of the Sun near the Horoscope; and the Nocturnal Planets, as Mars, Venus, Luna, and Mercury, are in Nocturnal Houses in the West and Occidental of the Sun; especially near the cusp of the seventh. The fourth is when the three Superiors, Saturn, Jupiter or Mars, are in Masculine Quarters; which are counted from the cusp of the tenth House to the cusp of the Ascendant, and from the cusp of the fourth House to the cusp of the seventh House; and when the Feminines, viz., Venus or the Moon are in Feminine Quarters, which are from the cusp of the Ascendant to the cusp of the fourth House, and from the cusp of the seventh to the cusp of the tenth. As for Mercury, he delights when with Masculine Planets in Masculine Quarters, but with Feminine Planets in Feminine.

9. THE 9TH consideration is to take notice of the several ways, as well secret as manifest, good and evil, whereby things are helped or hindered to be done or not done, and of these there are one-and-twenty in number. 1. A most strong secret Helper. 2. A very strong secret Helper. 3. A strong secret Helper. 4. A weak secret Helper. 5. A weaker secret Helper. 6. A most weak secret Helper. 7. A most strong mani-

fest Helper. 8. A very strong manifest Helper. 9. A strong manifest Helper. 10. A weak manifest Helper. 11. A weaker manifest Helper. 12. A most weak manifest Helper. 13. A most strong secret Hinderer. 14. A very strong secret Hinderer. 15. A strong secret Hinderer. 16. A weak secret Hinderer. 17. A weaker secret Hinderer. 18. A most weak secret Hinderer. 19. A most strong manifest Hinderer. 20. A very strong manifest Hinderer; and 21. A strong manifest Hinderer. All which we shall treat particularly, the same being a secret of secrets. In the judicial part of Astrology which the Ancients did not regard, nor have said anything plainly of it that I find, save only that Haly seems to have touched a little upon it in his Exposition of the 23d of Ptolemy's *Centiloquium*; nor do I believe they omitted those things out of ignorance, but rather through disuse or fear of being too tedious, or burdening the minds of their Readers or Auditors. For they were wont to judge, according as they found the Planets disposed in Houses and Signs, their Fortitudes and Debilities, together with the Part of Fortune, and some few other things. But thou oughtest to consider in thy Judgments, not only what they did, but also all other circumstances that thou canest; for when thou dost erect a figure, thou shouldest first find the Significator of the thing enquired after, or to be undertaken, and see if any of the fixed stars of his own Nature be in either of his Houses, or in his Exaltation, or in conjunction with him to a minute; for then such star shall so far help the significator, that the thing shall be accomplished and effected, even beyond the Querent's hopes, and this is a most strong secret Helper, for the Querent may well wonder how it comes to pass. Now, if the same star should be in the same degree with the Significator from one minute to 15 minutes before him or 5 minutes behind him, it will still help him, but not so much; and this we call a very strong secret Helper; but if it be with him in the same degree, but above 16 minutes distance and within 50 minutes, it will somewhat help, yet this less; and this we call in the Positive degree only a strong secret Helper. If it be in the same degree with the Significator, in a place where he has two of his smaller Dignities, in the very same minute, or within 16 minutes, it will help him yet less, and then 'tis a weak secret Helper; from 16 minutes to 50 minutes still less, and then 'tis a weaker secret Helper; but if it be with the significator in a place where he has no dignities at all it will still help, but as it were insensibly; and this we call a most weak secret Helper. The like we may say on the contrary of those things that prejudice, frustrate, and hinder business, for if a Planet which is a Significator of anything, being in a place where he has not any Dignities, shall be joined with one of the Fixed Stars of a contrary nature, it will weaken him and not suffer the thing to come to pass; although otherwise by the Figure it seemed never so probable; so that, for want of heeding this, the Artist often gets discredit, and raises a scandal on the Art itself amongst the ignorant; and this is a most strong secret Hinderer; whereas if the same star be remote above 16 minutes from the Significator, it will weaken him, but not altogether so much; whence it may be called only a very strong secret Hinderer. And so downwards through all degrees in the same manner as we said of the Helpers or Assistant Causes respectively.

Of the 21 several Modes aforesaid, which are most strong Helpers, etc., and which strongest obstructs.

The several Modes before mentioned are thus to be known and distinguished. A most strong manifest Helper or Adjuvant cause is when the Planet which is Significator of a thing is in his own House; in an Angle on the very minute of the Cusp, direct, swift of course, in reception, and free from all affliction and impediment; which most seldom happens.

A strong manifest Helper, is when the Significator is in an Angle in his House or Exaltation, within 3 degrees before the Cusp, or 5 degrees after it.

A weak manifest Helper, is where a Planet is in two of his lesser Dignities in an Angle within 5 degrees before or 15 degrees after it; or is in his House, or Exaltation, in a succedent House free from Affliction.

A weaker open Helper, is when the Significator is in his own House or Exaltation, or two of his lesser Dignities, but in a cadent House of the Figure, yet beholding the Ascendant. A most weak open Helper is when the Significator is in some of his greater Dignities or two of his lesser, not beholding the Ascendant; or in one of his lesser Dignities; only beholding the same, or joined to a Planet that beholds the same, and has some Dignities therein.

A most strong open Hinderer is when the Significator is in a place where he hath no Dignity, no delight, is not received; besieged by the Two Infortunes, Cadent from an Angle, and from the Ascendant, and so much the worse if joined with any of the Fixed Stars, of a mischievous nature, etc.

There may be other both adjuvant and obstructing causes, besides what we have mentioned, both open and secret; proceeding from the conjunctions of Planets and their Aspects, too tedious here to discourse of. Nor shall I here enlarge on all those before mentioned, but must assure thee that this ninth consideration, carefully observed, will be of great use in raising a true and wary judgment; especially if thou hast always a diligent eye to the Moon; for she of all the Planets has the greatest similitude and correspondence with Inferior things, both in general and particular, as well the species of the kinds as the individuals of the species; with winds; to pass by her daily effects which she causes in all things here, and frequent revolutions about the Elements and Elementary Bodies by reason of the nearness of her Orb to the Earth, and smaller circle than any other Planet; so that she seems a Mediatrix between Superior and Interior Bodies.

And as we see that in the New Moon she appears small and thin, and little, but afterwards her light gradually increases, till all that part of her body towards us becomes replenished with luster; and then again it decays by insensible degrees till she totally disappears, just so do all bodies both of things Rational, Irrational, and Vegetative as men grow until they are completed to their determinate stature, and then droop and decline continually till their life is ended; and so of all other things. Hence 'tis necessary to mate the Moon concerned in the signification of every Question, Nativity, Enterprise and Business, and her good condition to show the good issue of the thing, and so on the contrary. For her Virtue and Power is such and so great, that if the Lord of the Ascendant or other Significator of a business be so weak and afflicted that he cannot bring it about and complete it as he ought; if she be but strong it shall, notwithstanding, be accomplished. For she is the School-mistress of all things; the Bringer-down of all the Planets' influences, and a kind of an "internuncio" between them, carrying their virtues from one to the other, by receiving the disposition of one planet end bearing it to another. And some have thought that she does this at all times, of which opinion was that Tyrant Cylinus de

Romano, viz., that when she separates from one Planet, she takes the virtue and carries it to another, committing the same to the first that she can meet with. And some have imagined that Zael said the same; but his meaning was not absolutely so; for he believed that the Moon did bear what was committed to her; but if it were not so given or committed to her she could not carry anything to any; to which I assent, for when the Moon is joined to any planet that receives her, then that planet commits its disposition to her, who carries it with her and bestows it on that planet whom she first meets with in any of her dignities, and not to another, according to that Aphorism—"A planet gives nothing in a place where he has promised nothing."

10. THE 10TH consideration is warily to observe what Fixed Stars may either help or hinder the matter in question; for they have oftentimes great power, and lead the Astrologer sometimes into error; and let the Artist be sure to consider the places of the Fixed Stars, as they are in the present age carefully reduced.[1]

11. THE 11TH consideration is to take notice of the Malevolent Planets, and what they signify; for Saturn and Mars are naturally bad, Saturn for excess of cold, and Mars for excess of heat; not that either of them is really hot or cold, but virtually so; and these are their effects. And so they signify evil and damage and hindrance, unless they receive the Significator or the Moon by House, Exaltation, or two of their smaller Dignities; or shall themselves be Significators; for then they will bridle their malice, and not weaken or hinder him whom they receive, with what aspect soever they be-

---

[1] The longitudes of the fixed stars increase at the annual rate of 50.25".

hold him; but if they do not receive, their malice is increased; and so much the more it they be in Opposition or Square; for in Sextile or Trine the mischief is less. Yet Zael seems to say that the Infortunes lay aside or restrain their malice, where they are in Trine or Sextile; but his meaning was only that they were not then so violent, and intended not that their malice was wholly abated.

12. THE 12TH consideration is to behold the Fortunes, and see what they signify; for Jupiter and Venus are Fortunes by Nature, and being temperate, are said to be without any malice, because they do hurt to none, unless now and then by accident; which is beside their intention and profitably, and always endeavor to help both their own and others, whether they receive them or not; but so much the better if they receive them; and their Trine or Sextile is better and more advantageous than their Square, and their Square than their Oppositions.

13. THE 13TH consideration is to regard the Sun and his Significators, for he is also called a fortune, and so, whatever aspect he shall be beheld by, unless it be Opposition; but by Conjunction he becomes an Infortune, because then he renders every star that is so in Conjunction with him, combust and unfortunate; unless the same shall be in the heart of the Sun, and there every star is fortified.

14. THE 14TH consideration is to mind Mercury and the Moon, and what Planets they are joined with; because they will have the same significations with those with whom they are so joined; being of a convertible nature.

15. THE 15TH consideration is to regard the several ways in general whereby Planets make impressions on these infe-

rior things, which are two, one good and the other bad; for the Fortunes have power of imprinting good naturally, and the Infortunes as naturally shower down ill impressions; whence thou mayest, wherever thou seest the Fortunes, hope for good; and when thou beholdest the Malevolents, fear mischief, unless the same be restrained as aforesaid.

16. THE 16TH consideration is to take notice whether the Planet that is Significator of anything, be afflicted by either of the Malevolents; which is when one of them casts his rays upon the rays of such Significators, according to the quantity of their Orbs; and whilst he so continues with his rays or light under those of the Malevolent, such Significator is said to be impeded, hindered or afflicted, till the Malevolent have passed him; and Zael says, "After the ill Planet has passed the Planet he did afflict, one whole degree the Planet shall be said to be freed from him."[2] But rather I think that after the Malevolent is passed him one minute, he may be said to be free and excepted; for afterwards he can only frighten him. True it is he raises a greater fear when he is past him only one minute, than when he is gone by a whole degree; but yet even then it is such a kind of fear as is net altogether without some glimmering of hope. As thus, One intending to go into a Battle, inquires whether he shall return from thence safe and sound or not. And the Ascendant is Gemini 13 degrees, and Mercury in the 7th degree and 54 minutes of Aquary, in the IXth joined with Saturn, who is likewise in 7 degrees 53 minutes of Aquary, so that Mercury is now separated from Saturn, who was Lord of the House of Death, one minute; whence it appears that he should have died in that engagement by reason of the Conjunction, and was in peril of death and a kind of desperate fear that he should be slain by his ene-

---

[2] This can apply only in Horary Astrology.

mies and shall be pursued by them so that he shall seem not able to escape, and they shall often lay hands on him, but at last he shall get from them and make his escape; even beyond his own hopes; and all because Mercury is separated from Saturn; and Zael saith, "That if a Malevolent planet that would hinder any business be cadent from the Ascendant so that he cannot behold it, he cannot really hinder the matters; but only puts the persons concerned into terrors and frights about it."

17. THE 17TH consideration is to view whether the Planet that is Significator, be safe and prosperous, that is, free from any affliction from the Infortunes; and one of the Fortunes casts his beams or light on the beams of such Significator; for then shall that Planet be said to be safe and guarded till the Fortune is passed by the space of one minute, and signifies the perfection of the thing. But after he has passed him one minute, it will not be perfected or accomplished; for it only raises hopes; as (we said) the Malevolent in the like case could do nothing, but create fear. Yet is such a hope as the Querent will believe and fancy himself as it were certain; yet not without something of doubt; as for example, a Question is proposed of some weighty and difficult business, whether it will be done and brought to pass or not and 17 degrees of Scorpio ascends, and Mars is 12 degrees 13 minutes of Taurus, and Venus in 12 degrees and 14 minutes of Capricorn, so that Venus is joined to Mars by a Trine, and receives him in her House, who likewise receives her in his Exaltation; so that the Querent thinks, and all others concerned verily believe, that it would be accomplished by that aspect of perfect friendship; in which flattering hopes they continue till Venus hath passed the Aspect of Mars one whole degree; but at last the business comes to just nothing at all, because

Venus was past Mars one minute at the time of the Question proposed. Yet may a thing possibly in such a case be brought to pass, but not without extraordinary labor and trouble. And here likewise Zael affirms, "That if the Fortune be cadent from the Ascendant, so that it cannot behold the same, it only flatters with splendid hopes, but never completes the business."

18. THE 18TH consideration is to take notice when a Planet is in the Angles of the Infortunes, for unless these receive him there, he shall be said to be in an ill condition, and in straits and troubles; as a man on whom some have made an assault; who has many to combat with and nine to assist and take his part; or like one that strives against the stream, or falls into a deep pool, and knows not how to swim; and yet by thrusting out his hands and feet, may obtain the bank and escape; though this seldom happens. Now a Planet is said to be in the Angles of a Malevolent, when the Malevolent or Infortune, viz., Saturn or Mars, is in one sign, and the other Planet in the fourth, seventh or tenth from him; as if Mars be in Aries, and Mercury in Cancer, Libra, or Capricorn, he is said to be in his Angles, understand the like of their Corporal Conjunction. But if there be a Reception, he does not afflict; for reception abates all malice, as we have said elsewhere.

19. THE 19TH consideration is to behold the Moon it she be void of course, for then it signifies an impediment to the thing in question. It will net come to a good end, nor be accomplished; but the Querent shall be forced to desist with shame and loss.

20. THE 20TH consideration is to observe whether the Moon or Significator be joined to any of the Planets, for thence you must derive your judgment of what is like to hap-

pen in the business. Take notice therefore whether the planet to which the Moon or Significator joins, receives them; for then there will be a good laudable end; and the matter will be accomplished with success, if the receiver be a Fortune. But if there reception, yet if the Moon or Significator shall give virtue to that planet, the thing will still come to pass. But if it be an Infortune, though they do not give him virtue, yet without a reception it will not do; but with a reception, if he be not afflicted, it signifies a good end of the matter, though not without much labor and tediousness.

21. THE 21ST consideration is to see from what planet the Moon separates, for that signifies what is past of the business, as from a Fortune the good, from an Infortune the ill that hath been.

22. THE 22D consideration is to note which of the planets the Moon is now joined to, for that signifies what is now present; and from thence we must judge of the present state of the matter.

23. THE 23D consideration is to behold to whom the Moon is now joining[3], so as her Conjunction is not yet completed, for that signifies what is to come; wherefore if thou wouldest judge of a thing, which as yet is not, but 'tis hoped will hereafter be brought to pass, 'tis necessary then thou shouldest see to whom the Moon will next join; and according to her Significations judge whether good or evil.

24. THE 24TH consideration is to note whether the planet who is significator, be in his Declension, for then it causes a hindrance to everything thereby signified, and trouble and

---

[3] Or by applying aspect.

grief about it; and if the Question be about a prison wherein the Querent fears he shall be put, it signifies he shall be cast into the same together with disgrace and prejudice; and if the Question concerns one already in prison, it signifies a tedious confinement and more affliction than he believes.

25. THE 25TH consideration is whether the Planet that is Significator be Retrograde, or Stationary to Retrogradation, for then it signifies mischief and damage, discord, contradiction, and going backward with damage; yet being Stationary is not so bad as being Retrograde. For the last notes the mischief to be, as it were, present and in being. But being Stationary notes that 'tis past and over.

26. THE 26TH consideration is whether the Significator be in his Second Station, that is towards Direction, for that signifies also hindrance and evil, which already hath been and is past; yet some say that this Second Station is as good as direction, but this is only a way of speaking, as when one hath been sick and begins to grow well, we say he is recovered and sound, which is not simply true, but somewhere near it; for as the First Station is not so bad as Retrogradation, so the Second Station is not so good as direction.

27. THE 27TH consideration is whether the Infortunes are the Significators of anything, for if they signify ill, the evil will be much augmented, and if good it will be much diminished, abated, imperfect, and with difficulty; so that the party will scarce think his business done, unless by chance they be in a very good condition and excellently disposed.

28. THE 28TH consideration is whether the Significator be slow of Course, for then it delays the effect; and if it be in the beginning of anything, retards it, so that it will scarce ever

be finished; besides, things proceed slowly, where Significators are pointed in Sagittary, Capricorn, Aquary or Pisces, or who are the Lords of them, whether they be slow of Course; in Aries or Scorpio they are not quite so dilatory. In Leo they hasten business; more in Taurus or Libra; but most at all in Gemini or Virgo.

29. THE 29TH consideration is whether the Moon be joined to any planet by body or aspect exactly to a minute; for that signifies the present state of things; and from that minute observe what planet she joins next, for he shall be Significator of all that shall happen of that thing; as the planet she was last before with, was of what has already passed as aforesaid.

30. THE 30TH consideration is to observe when a planet that is Significator, or the Moon, shall have passed the 29th degree of the Sign wherein it is, and touches the 30th, and especially if it has passed one minute of that degree; for then it shall have no strength in that Sign, but in the next; so that if in the first it signified any evil, it shall hurt the person or thing threatened no more than the fall of a house shall one that is just got out of it; or being with one foot upon the threshold, has one behind him that throws him out, and then the building falls. And if it signified any good, it shall profit no more than he that hath spread a net for birds, and just touches the feathers of their tails, but never catches their bodies; and therefore Zael says, "If a planet or the Moon be in the 29th degree of any Sign, its virtue is yet in that Sign wherein he is; because he has not yet wholly past the 29th degree."

31. THE 31ST consideration is to look when one planet applies to the Conjunction of another. If he be near the end of the same Sign wherein he is himself, or that other to whom he

applies; so that he will pass out of that Sign before the Conjunction is perfected; and to see if he be joined with him in the following Sign to which he is changed, because then the cause is perfected; if that planet confers anything on him in that Sign wherein he is so joined to him; that is, if any reception happen, unless the said planet, or he to whom he applies, be first joined to another; for then the business comes to nothing, and will not be perfected, though he be joined again to the other interposed before the first Conjunction is accomplished. Nor must it be forgotten that a Corporal Conjunction forbids an Aspect and cuts it off, but an Aspect cannot do so by a Conjunction.

32. THE 32D consideration is if an Infortune be the Significator, what his condition is; for if it be good, there will good come of the thing; if bad, rather evil; as Sarviator says in *Pentadera*, "An ill-planet strong in his own Home or Exaltation, Not joined with any other Infortune to impede or waken him, is better than a Fortune Retrograde afflicted."

33. THE 33D consideration is to see whether either of the Infortunes be the Significator of anything, and be joined to another Infortune impeding him, or has joined to him the Lord of the Ascendant or the Moon, by a Square or Opposition; for then this Infortune will perfect the business, but the business will not be good, or rather It will be destroyed after it seems perfected. But if the Infortune that impedes be the lighter of the two, so that he apply to a Conjunction, with the Significator, it will hinder less than if the Significator apply to the other.

34. THE 34TH consideration is to mind in Questions or Nativities, whether the Significator of the business be an Infortune and Lord of the Ascendant, and in the Ascendant; di-

rect, not vitiated, and in good condition; for then he would both affect the same and bring it to a good conclusion; nay, although he be not Significator nor Lord of the Ascendant, but only be in the Ascendant, and that the same be his Exaltation; he lays aside all his malice, and is restrained from mischief; but if he be weak and afflicted, his malice and contrariety is increased so as to destroy the business wholly.

35. THE 35TH consideration is to look whether an Infortune be in Signs like him, or of his own nature, for that abates his ill effects; like a cross fellow when he is pleased and has what he will, as Saturn in Capricorn, Aquary, or Libra, or in a cold Sign, especially if he have any Dignifies there, and so Mars in Aries, Scorpio, Capricorn, or a hot Sign, etc. But if Saturn be in a hot Sign, or Mars in a cold Sign, out of their dignities, it will be bad, and the business be no more completed than oil will mix with water; but if strong and well disposed, they will mix in good, like water and wine, or milk with honey.

36. THE 36TH consideration is to observe when the Infortunes are the obstructors of a business, whether the Fortunes behold them with a Trine or Sextile Aspect; for then their ill nature will be allayed and mitigated; but much more if these receive them.

37. THE 37TH consideration is to look if the Fortunes are the Significators, whether the Infortunes behold them with Opposition or Square; for that will much lessen their kind effects, and diminish the good they otherwise promised.

38. THE 38TH consideration is to consider if the Fortunes are Significators, whether they are Cadent from Angles, or from the Ascendant, so as not to behold the same,

and be Retrograde; for under these impediments they will be almost as bad as the Infortunes themselves, unless they be in reception.

39. THE 39TH is to consider if the Significator be in Reception; for if it be a Fortune, its signification will thereby be much bettered, and its impediment and mischief much lessened if it be an Infortune.

40. THE 40TH is to consider if an Infortune, whether he be Significator or not, be Peregrine; that is, not in any of his Dignities, for then his malice is increased; but when in his Dignities it somewhat abates it; that is in his House, Exaltation, or Terms; but in his Triplicity or Face very little, and in Hayz least of all.

41. THE 41ST is if an Infortune, being significator, be in his own House or Exaltation, or in his own Terms or Triplicity, or in Angles or Succedent Houses; for by all these means he is fortified, and shall be counted strong as a Fortune.

42. THE 42D is if a Fortune be Significator, or give virtue or assistance to any of the Planets, and be in a House where he has none of the Lordly Dignities, then his good signification will be lessened and abated; and soon the contrary.

43. THE 43D is if the Fortunes and Infortunes be together ill-posited, that is, in some of the said impediments, as Houses where they have no Dignities, Combust or the like; then whatever they signify 'tis but weakly; according to that Aphorism of the Philosopher, "A Planet Retrograde and Combust, has no strength in signification. The Fortunes when Combust and under the Sun's beams, signify none or

very little good; and the Infortunes in like case have little or no virtue to signify ill."[4]

44. THE 44TH is to consider if the Significators, Fortune or Infortune, be in his own House, Exaltation, Triplicity, Terms or Face (but the latter being not of that virtue with the rest, 'tis necessary it should be assisted with another Dignity, which is Hayz or Light; for in such case the Infortune loses his sting; and being reined in like a wild horse from doing mischief, his malice is converted into good, and though this seems strange, yet the ancients affirm and I myself have often found it true by experience.

45. THE 45TH is to consider if Infortunes are in angles of the Ascendant, that is. In such signs as are in square or Opposition to the Ascendant, when they afflict any Planet by Square or Opposition; for then they assist so much the worse, and do more mischief, especially if they be in a stronger place than such afflicted Planet; but if they cast only a Trine or a Sextile, it is lessened and the impediment mitigated.

46. THE 46TH is to see whether the Significator be a Fortune or an Infortune, the first naturally signifies good and prosperity, the last naturally evil by its malignity; therefore consider the Planets' places from the Ascendant where they are; for if a Planet be in his Light, or his Hayz in any of his Dignities, or in a good place from the Ascendant, it signifies good; and if it be a good planet the better.

47. THE 47TH is to consider whether the significator be in his Light or no, that is a Diurnal Planet in the day, above the

---

[4] An Infortune should be regarded as having very evil signification under the circumstances.

earth, and in the night under the Earth; and a Nocturnal Planet in the night above the Earth, and in the day under it, to this renders such Planet more strong. But if a Nocturnal Planet be Significator of anything in the day above the Earth, or a Diurnal Planet in the night, the same is thereby weakened and under a kind of impediment, that he can scarce accomplish what he signified.

48. THE 48TH is to consider, when an Infortune is Significator and his ill effects are mitigated, whether Jupiter behold him, or is joined corporally to him, for that will wholly destroy his malignity and turn his nature into good, how bad soever he be; so that if Saturn in that place of himself would not bestow some good or perform what he seems to promise, Jupiter will make him do it, provided he be not afflicted himself, as in his fall, Combust or Retrograde (yet even then he helps, but not so powerfully). On the other side Venus takes off the fury of Mars, by reason of that endearing intimacy which is between them, unless the thing be very difficult, as wars and bloodshed, etc. But she cannot so well divert the mischief of Saturn without the help of Jupiter (and then she can do it as well as at other times that of Mars). The reason is, there is no such sympathy between Saturn and she, in any respect; for he is slow, she swift; he heavy, she light; he delights in melancholy, she in mirth.

49. THE 49TH is to consider whether one of the Infortunes being Significator, be joined to another, for if he signified a good himself, this will destroy or frustrate it; but if any evil, it will augment and double it, or change it into some worse mischief of another kind; as when the pain near the navel turns into a dry Dropsy; but if joined to a Fortune with a reception on either side, the evil will be converted into good; but with-

out a Reception it will only be allayed and abated, according to the strength of such Fortune.

50. THE 50TH is to observe the Lord of the Ascendant and the Moon, whether they or either of them are afflicted by either of the Infortunes, by Conjunction, Opposition, or Square, the business will be spoiled without the aspect of a Fortune, but if a Fortune, that is, Jupiter, Venus, the Sun or Moon shall behold them, it slackens and dissolves the rigors of such Infortune, and the party signified shall be freed from the danger impending, although the aspect be a Square, provided it be with Reception); but if a Fortune without Reception, by a Square or Opposition, or an Infortune with a Trine or Sextile without Reception, shall behold the said Lord of the Ascendant, 'tis possible the party may be delivered from the present danger; but it will be turned into another as great, so that it will not profit him.

51. THE 51ST is to see whether the Significator be cadent from an Angle or from the Ascendant, and in none of his Dignities, nor in his Joy; for then he signifies nothing but doubts and mischiefs, and there are no hopes of good or profit from a planet so disposed.

52. THE 52D is when the three Inferiors, Venus, Mercury, and Luna, come from under the rays of the Sun, and appear in the evening after his setting, for before (viz., till they are got from him 12 degrees) they, or any other planet, are weak, so that a Fortune can advantage little, and an Infortune prejudice as much. Now if the Fortune come forth slow in motion, as with labor, then will not the good expected be obtained without much pains and trouble; and if it be an Infortune, his signification will appear slowly. But in the Superiors, as Saturn, Jupiter, and Mars, these things happen when they come from

under the Sun beams, that they rise in the morning before the Sun, and shine before his rising.

53. THE 53D consideration is whether the significator be under the Sun beams, for then he will be of small efficacy in anything as aforesaid; yet the Malevolents will be something more strong in evil than the Benevolents in goal.

Note by Lilly—"Now a planet is properly said to be under the Sun beams, when there are only 12 degrees or less, or above, or 16 minutes distance between it and the Sun; for when there is only 16 minutes distance, it is said to be strong, being in Cazimi, or the heart of the Sun[5]; but when there are more than 12 degrees and less than 15 degrees, it is said to be going from under the Sun's beams."

54. THE 54TH is to consider whether a superior planet be removed 12 degrees from the Sun, going to his morning rising, or an Inferior is so much, and direct, going to his evening rising, for then he is said to be fortified; but when he is got 15 degrees, so that he appears, he is more fortified in everything; like one coming out of a battle rejoicing having destroyed and pouted all his enemies. But when the Sun follows the three Superiors, and there shall be between them and him less than 15 degrees, their weakness is said to be increased, until there shall be only 7 degrees between them and afterwards, until they shall be in the heart of the Sun, they are said to be in extreme debility; but the debility of the Inferiors is contrary to them, for it is said to be increased when they follow the Sun, and that there is between them and the Sun from 15 degrees to 7 degrees, and from 7 degrees till they are in the heart

---

[5] This fortitude is very doubtful. A planet so situated should be regarded as in the worst state of Combustion.

of the Sun, they are said to be in their greatest debility.

55. THE 55TH is to consider whether the significator be Peregrine, for then the person whom he signifies, either in a Nativity or Question, etc., will be subtle, crafty, malicious, one that shall know how to act both good and evil, but more inclined to the latter.

56. THE 56TH is to consider if the significator of anything shall commit his disposition or virtue to any other Planet whether it be to one that is Oriental or Occidental, for if he be Oriental and one of the Inferiors and direct, or if he be Occidental and one of the Superiors, and that there be not above 20 minutes between him and the Sun, he will be weak, says Sarcinator, and not perform what he shows, but hinders many things; under that impediment, like a sick man whose disease has prevailed so far that he is forced to lie by it and cannot help himself; or a falling house which none can preserve from ruin; and so much further as such Planet shall be from the Sun, so much less shall he be afflicted. And if it be Oriental and one of the Superiors, or Occidental and one of the Inferiors, and not Retrograde, he shall be strong and fit to perfect what he promises; as one that hath been ill, but is more perfectly recovered, or a building which fell and is repaired, and so of all other planets so disposed.

57. THE 57TH is to consider whether the significator be in the Eighth from the Ascendant, for if he be there, and a Fortune, though he do not harm, he will do no good; and if he be an Infortune he will do greater mischief than in any other place of the Figure; and if the Question be of going to War, advise not the Querent to go there, although it be a Fortune; for always some evil is to be suspected, that is death, or at least captivity, for it is a place of darkness and death; but if it

be an Infortune, judge death, unless he separate then from the Lord of the Eighth; for then it may be only a wound, or bruise, or a fall, wherein he was in danger of death, although he may escape; and if it be a journey, especially a long one, he will be taken prisoner, or in great dread of it; understand still if he separate from the Lord of the Eighth; and also remember that an Infortune so disposed always does more mischief than a Fortune.

58. THE 58TH is to consider whether the Significator be fixed in that Sign where he is found? Now Zael saith, "That a Planet is not said to be fixed in a Sign till he hath passed 5 degrees thereof." But I am of opinion that when he hath passed one whole degree of a Sign he is firmly therein, but he said it for more certainty. So likewise he says, "That a Planet is not said to be cadent from the Ascendant unless he be removed from thence 5 degrees; as, for example, the Ascendant in 9 degrees of Aries, and a Planet was in the fifth degree thereof, Ptolemy and many other sages affirm that Planet to be in an Angle, with whom I agree; yet some would have it that a Planet should be said to be in an angle when he is in the very degree of the Ascendant, or one degree before it or two after it; but they meant in Revolutions, and that they might be so certain as not to be in the least deceived. But I have experienced that a Planet is in an Angle to the space of 5 degrees beyond the cusp; for as once I sought the Revolution of a year, I found Mars in the 5th degree beyond the cusp of the Angle of the Earth in Capricorn, South Latitude, which signified the killing of the Roman emperor; and acquainted him with it, for his court was at Grossietti and I at Forlirii; and it was found that Pandulfus de Farsenella and Theobaldus Franciscus, and diverse others of the secretaries had conspired to slay him, and none of his own Astrologers observed it, because they

did net believe that Mars was in an Angle, for he was 4 degrees beyond the cusp and 58 minutes in their opinion; however, after a Planet shall be removed from the cusp or line of any Angle full 5 degrees or more, he is to be counted Cadent from that Angle."

59. THE 59TH is to consider whether the significator be behind the cusp of an Angle 15 degrees and no more; for he shall be said to be in an Angle as well as he that is exactly there, as Gael affirms; whence he said before that it was not in an Angle, nor had any strength there beyond the 15th degree after the cusp of the Angle; for example, the Ascendant is 4 degrees of Taurus, and the end thereof was behind the Angle, whatever planet is posited from the 4th to the 19th degree thereof is in the angle, but what is beyond that is not; but Ptolemy seems to intimate, though he says not expressly, "that every planet who shall be 5 degrees before, or 25 degrees after the cusp, is in the Angle." Now Zael would clear the doubt, lest that great distance of the planet from the Angle should hinder the business.

Note by Lilly—"The same Ptolemy (from whom I cannot differ) seems to assert that no part of any House remains void of virtue; and myself am of opinion, I think not idly, that every planet that is in any House shall be said to be in that House, where he is found, from the beginning of the House, even to the end thereof; and therefore I say in the House, not in the Sign, because sometimes the same House comprehends more than one Sign and sometimes less; for it seems ridiculous that any part of any House should continue idle, and be left void of virtue."

60. THE 60TH is to consider whether the significator be in a Sign fixed, common, or moveable; because in a fixed Sign

he signifies stability and countenance of the thing begun, or to be undertaken, or enquired of. In a common Sign, a change with a return or repeating of it, that the same will once be broken off, and afterwards begun again, or something added, or other alteration happen; for which reason in things that require alteration, as buying, selling, or the like, we should put the Significator and Moon, or one of them, into a common Sign; but in a moveable Sign it signifies a sudden change, a quick despatch or end whether good or evil. And therefore in matters where we desire a sudden conclusion, we ought to put the significator in moveable Signs; but things that we desire should be fixed and endure, we ought to place them in fixed Signs; where we would have a mean, let them be in common Signs. Understand the same always of the nature of the Moon, if at any time thou canest observe it.

61. THE 61ST is to behold whether the Lord of the Ascendant or Moon be with the Dragon's Head or Tail; for that is an impediment in all affairs, and the hindrance or mischief will proceed from a cause signified by that House the Dragon's Head or Tail hurts, unless it be corporal for they have no Aspect or Opposition. And it is worse when the Significator or Moon goes towards them, than when they go from them; for in the first case is signified the mischief in its full height, like a man in a ship that is split in the sea, when there is no hope. But in the last, 'tis like a ship that is only in danger, but has hopes and probabilities of escaping. And note that when the significator or Moon goes to the Dragon's Head, its malice is augmented, for its nature is to increase, and when they go to the Tail, the mischief is not absolutely at the worst, as 'tis when they go from it, that is, within one degree; for from one degree forwards 'tis not so great as in that degree, although much; and from 1 degree to 3 degrees less, and from 3 de-

grees to 5 degrees yet less, and from 5 degrees to 7 degrees very small; from 7 degrees to 9 degrees smaller, and from thence to 12 degrees little or nothing at all.

62. THE 62D is to consider whether the Moon be void of course, for that signifies that the thing enquired after shall scarce ever come to a good end, or not without much labor, sorrow, and trouble, unless the Lord of the Ascendant or significator of the thing shall be in very good condition, and then it may be hindered, but not wholly frustrated; yet 'tis a good time then for drinking, battling, feasting, etc., and to use ointments for taking away of hair, especially if she be in Scorpio.

63. THE 63D is to consider whether the Moon be far from the Conjunction of the Infortunes, so as not to cast her beams on theirs, for then the event will be good, but rather if she touch with her beams those of the Fortunes. And yet better, if besides this the Lord of the Ascendant, or of the business, be in good condition; for if they be not well disposed, it may impair the good promised, but not wholly prevent it.

64. THE 64TH is to consider whether the Moon be in Cancer, Taurus, Sagittarius, or Pisces; for it signifies good in the business, although she be joined to the Infortunes and not to the Fortunes; nor does she, being void of course, prejudice so much in those places as elsewhere, provided she be not Combust, for then they will advantage her little or northing.

65. THE 65TH is to consider whether the Lord of the Seventh is afflicted or not, for that will be an impediment to the business. And you ought to defer judgment if you can, and warily search always whence such impediment shall arise, as well by the Conjunction of the Lord of the Seventh with the

Planets, as by their separation, and also of the Moon; so mayest thou find whence it will proceed, and afterwards give judgment with more safety.

66. THE 66TH is to consider when the Infortunes threaten mischief, whether the place on which their threats fall be the Dignity of any of the Fortunes and whether then it will take away the mischief and annul it wholly. If by a Square, it will only lessen it; if by an Opposition, take away some part of it; but if it cast no aspect at all, the mischief will happen; but it will proceed from honest, just persons, and it may be the Querent suffers rightfully, being cast in a just cause before a Judge, or the like. But if the aforesaid place be the Dignity of an Infortune, the prejudice will come from unjust men, false witnesses, a corrupt Judge, or some sentence unjustly given through a mistake, etc.

67. THE 67TH is to consider whether there be any Eclipse near, which is less than 12 degrees from the Significator, for the same will bring damage and mischief to the Querent or business unless there be there a Fortune which hath Dignities in the same place, for then the same is abated; but if there be no such, thou oughtest to look what Planet beholds the said place of the Eclipse and how. For if the Fortunes behold it, they do but augment the evil; and if they are Infortunes, they lessen and abate it, which seems a kind of riddle or wonder in Art.

68. THE 68TH is to consider in questions relating to sick people, or Decumbitures, whether the Lord of the Seventh, and Seventh House itself, be free from impediments, for if they be, the sick may safely trust himself to the care of the Physicians, for medicines will do very well. But if the Seventh House and its Lord shall be Afflicted, Ptolemy saith, "The Physician must be changed, for neither his physic nor

care will do any good"; for the seventh signifies the medicine as Zael saith, or at least the disease grows chronical and lasting. The like is to be expected if the same positions happen at the beginning of any cure.

69. THE 69TH is to consider whether the significators of the Ascendant, and of the House signifying the thing enquired be of equal strength and debility, for then thou canest not safely give judgment; but in such case thou must mind the Lord of the Conjunction or Prevention (as the thing is either conjunctional or preventional) which was last before, and by that judge, but if the Lord of the Conjunction or Prevention, and of the things, be still equal, thou must then turn to the Moon, and see to whom she first applies, and thence deduce judgment. If she join not to any in or from the Sign in which she is, take that with whom she joins first in the next Sign, and this is very considerably useful.

70. THE 70TH consideration is to mind another secret; not well searched into by Astrologers, but often times doing them much prejudice; that is, see in all Questions, etc., whether the Lord of the New or Full Mom, preventional last before, be in any of the Angles of the thing enquired after; if it be, it denotes that the business will be accomplished, unless it be the Querent's own fault (or that God overrule against it), though perhaps by other significations it seemed not likely. But if it shall not happen so, but only the same is in the Ascendant; and the other significators, that is, the Lord of the Ascendant of the thing enquired of, and the Moon, or any of them assist, the thing will be done with ease. If it be in Cadent Houses, it will scarce ever be, though other significators seem never so favorable; and if two at least of them be not so, take it for certain it will never be done.

71. THE 71ST is to consider whether the significator falls between the Ascendant and the Twelfth, for that signifies continuance or length of time, when a thing will be done; or if done already, how long it will continue in days or hours. If between the twelfth and the tenth, it notes half weeks; between the tenth and seventh, months or weeks; between the seventh and fourth, years; and between the Fourth and the Ascendant, half years.[6]

---

[6] With regard to the measure of tine, the late Commander Morrison, R.N., writes, "The most difficult thing in all questions is to judge of time with accuracy. I should advise extreme caution in giving any judgment on this head, unless where it is the chief point desired to be known. In this case and if the figure be very radical, and if the planet which is applying to the other be taken, the following rule will hold good:

Each Degree gives:
In Moveable Signs and Angles . . . Days.
In Common Signs and Angles . . . Weeks.
In Fixed Signs and Angles . . . Months.

Succedent houses give weeks, months and years, as the sign is moveable, common or fixed; and cadent houses give months in moveable signs, years in common signs, and an indefinite time in fixed signs."

Dr. Simmonite, whose Astrological works are well known, writes, "It is generally very difficult to judge of time with accuracy. The limitation of time is taken either by house and sign, or by aspect. To ascertain the number of days, weeks, months, or years, consider the degree and minutes between the body or aspect of the significators, and according to the number of degrees which are between their aspect, even so many days, weeks, months, or years will it be before the matter enquired after is accomplished or destroyed. Observe in what house or sign the applying significator falls. Succedent houses give weeks, months, or years, as the sign is moveable, common, or fixed, and cadent houses give months in moveable signs, years in common, and unknown in fixed signs. Great south latitude prolongs the time; great north latitude often cuts it shorter; if the significators have no latitude, the exact time is made simply by the aspects. Degrees and minutes of latitude, if it be south, should, it is said,

72. THE 72D is to observe that if the question be of a journey, and the Moon afflicted, it is not safe to undertake it; but if it cannot be put off, make the Planet that afflicts her Lord of the Ascendant at the time of the Querent's setting forth.

73. THE 73D is to mind whether the Question signify good or evil. If good, whether the Fortunes behold the Significator of the Question, or the Moon, for then the good Fortune thereof will be increased; but if the Infortunes cast in their beams, as much or more diminished. But if it originally signify evil, and the Infortunes behold the significator or Moon, as aforesaid, the evil threatened will be increased and become much worse.

74. THE 74TH is to consider whether the Significator be in his first station, going to be Retrograde, for that signifies crossness and disobedience, and that the matter, though never so probable, will not be accomplished. If any work or building be then begun, it will not be finished. And it such Significator, so asserted, be then under the Earth, such building shall not be raised to any purpose in thirty years, and then not finished; and if it be raised a little then, it will be a raising thirty years more. And if not then completed, it will not be completed till ninety years after its first; and if not then, it will never be finished, unless the property be altered, and come into the possession of strangers from its former owners. But if the Significator be in his second station, going to be di-

---

be added to the time, but if north subtracted from it; as north latitude shortens the time of an event and south latitude lengthens it, but I have not much opinion of this. Transits show the progress of the matter and point out the most probable time in which the natter may be terminated; and that is the time to judge of. The good or evil days are those on which the transits are good or evil. Mixed application gives, instead of years, say months; for months, weeks; and for weeks, say days."

rect, it notes that the affair will be done, but slowly, intricately, and with pains and trouble. And if an edifice be then begun, it will be finished, but not so soon as was at first believed, provided the Significator be not under the Earth; for then he that begins it shall never make an end of it, nor raise it very high above the Earth.

Note by Lilly—"And note, a Planet in his second station signifies an aptness, and the renewing and strength of everything, but in his first station, dissolution and destruction. Remember and understand these things well, for they will often come in practice."

75. THE 75TH is to consider, whether the Moon be afflicted by any Planet, for then, whatever the question be, the same will suffer impediment. But if the Moon be in a good place from the Ascendant, so as to behold it with a Trine or Sextile, or if the Planet that afflicts her do behold the same, either of these Aspects will mitigate the mischief intended, and it may be, wholly take it away, as the said afflicting Planet is disposed; so that he be not Cadent from Angles, nor from the Ascendant, nor in his fall; that is with the seventh from his own House. Zael says "that if an Infortune afflicting be cadent from the Ascendant, or retrograde, it causeth fear in the Querent; but I always fear the affliction of the Moon above all other Impediments, and scarce remember that I ever saw a good end of anything where she was afflicted; and in journeys, if to war, was apprehensive of the Querent's care and person; if for traffic, of straits, quarrels, sadness in his travels, and loss of money, etc."

76. THE 76TH is to consider from what Planet the Moon separates, and which she is joined to; he whom she separates from signifies what hath been, the other what is to come, as

we have said. And therefore, if she separates from an Infortune, and applies to a Fortune, the worst is past; and what hitherto has been had, will end happily to the Querent's content. But if she separates from a Fortune, and goes to an Infortune, understand the contrary, the thing was good in the beginning, but proves naught in the end. If from a Fortune to a Fortune, it was and is good, and will have a laudable end. If from an Infortune to an Infortune, it will be an ugly conclusion.[7]

77. THE 77TH is to consider whether the Lord of the Ascendant or Moon be in Opposition, that is, whether the Moon be in Capricorn, Mercury in Sagittarius or Pisces, or Venus in Scorpio or Aries, the Sun in Aquarius, Mars in Taurus or Libra, Jupiter in Gemini or Virgo, Saturn in Cancer or Leo; for then such Lords of the Question abhor the business; nor does he love it should be accomplished, but is rather against it.

78. THE 78TH is to consider the house that signifies the thing whereof the Question is asked. For the First signifies the Person, the Second, substance, the Third, brethren, etc., as we have before taught, and as it shall appear, so judge having duly pondered all circumstances.

---

[7] This Consideration is in the doctrine of Translation. Translation of the light and nature of a planet when a planet separates from one that is slower than itself, and overtakes another either by conjunction or aspect. In horary astrology it is a good omen if the aspect be good; but if by an evil aspect, it is said to denote evil or difficulty when the event comes to pass. Thus, if a question of marriage a light planet translates the light of the Lord of the Seventh house to the Lord of the Ascendant, it is a good omen, if it be by good aspect, and denotes that a person answering the description of such translating planet will bring the parties together, and they will be eventually happy. If it be by evil aspect, it will be done either from ill motives or will be attended with much trouble and disappointment.

79. THE 79TH is to consider whether the significator, or Moon, be joined to good or ill planets, by Conjunction or by Aspect, which is diligently to be heeded and distinguished, for a corporal conjunction with the Sun is the greatest misfortune can befall a Planet.

80. THE 80TH is to consider how the Significator is posited in respect to his own House, whether in the second, third, or fourth, etc., sign from it, according to the Signification of that sign shalt thou judge, as thou would judge of any Planet in such a House from the Ascendant.

81. THE 81ST is to consider whether the Significator be in an Angle or in a Succedent or Cadent House, for how much any Planet is near to the cusp of any Angle so much is he the stronger; how much farther so much the weaker; and by how much sooner he shall be nearer the cusp of a Cadent House, so much shall he be the weaker; how much the farther, so much the less weak.

82. THE 82D is to consider whether the Significator receive disposition or virtue from any Planet, Fortune or Infortune. If from a Fortune it signifies good; and the better if such Fortune be in a good condition. If from an Infortune, to the contrary; and so much the worse by how much the more weak and affected he is.

83. THE 83D is to consider whether the Fortunes and Infortunes are equally strong in the Question; for that signifies no positive judgment, either good or ill; but a kind of indifference, and that the business will bring neither gain nor loss.

84. THE 84TH is to consider whether the Fortunes or Infortunes are strongest; for if both be strong, and the Fortunes

prevail in strength, it signifies a kind of mediocrity of good; if the Infortunes in such a case are strongest, a mediocrity of evil not in excess on either side.

85. THE 85TH is to consider whether the Part of Fortune fall in a good or bad place of the Figure; that is in an Angle, or in a Succedent or in a Cadent House; and how the same is aspected, and by when, a Fortune or an Infortune, and whether it be in reception of that Planet by whom it is aspected. For questions may sometimes seem good but the Part of Fortune happening in an untoward Place weakens it much and renders it less profitable so as to deceive the Querent's hopes. And on the contrary a question may seem ill, yet the Part of Fortune happening luckily, joined with a good Planet that receives it, etc., lessens the evil, and not so much happens to the Querent as the Figure otherwise seems to threaten.

86. THE 86TH is to consider whether either of the Infortunes behold the Significator both Retrograde, Cadent, Peregrine, and in signs contrary to their respective natures, for then they bring such an absolute mischief as cannot be avoided, nor averted by anything but God alone. And if any shall be born under such positions, he will always be a beggar, let him do what he can; or if any House be built then, no man shall ever live happily, or get money in it; but by losses and crosses his estates and goods shall moulder away, and come to nothing; and his most probable designs strangely frustrated and destroyed, unless the Divine Goodness in mercy interpose.

87. THE 87TH is to consider Novenarium Lunae, which is a thing much to be heeded, for it often hinders the Astrologer from discovering the truth, and leads him into error, not

knowing the cause that makes him deceive.

88. THE 88TH is to consider the Planet from whom not only the Moon separates, how he is disposed, etc., but the next to whom she is joined, so that there be not above 51 minutes distance between them, the first signifying what is past, the second what is now present, as we have already said, and also look to whom she will next be joined after separation from him with whom she is at present; for he will signify (according as he is disposed) the issue, or what is to come.

89. THE 89TH is to consider the Duodenariam Lunae, a thing very observable in many cases, even more than diverse things that we have said; for there is greatest danger of mistakes in abstruse considerations, and such as Astrologers rather through sloth than ignorance, do not regard; whereby they often fall into disgrace and contempt of the rabble, rather than take a little pains.

90. THE 90TH is to consider whether the Lord of the House in which the Sun is, and of that wherein the Moon is, and also the Lord of the Ascendant be all oriental and in Angles (though that rarely happens), and mutually behold each other from good places with friendly Aspect; for these positions shall signify the greatest good, and most superlative fortune imaginable. If they shall not be all so disposed, the remaining part shall signify prosperity and felicity proportionally as far as they are able, though not in so vast a measure.

91. THE 91ST consideration is to observe in Questions or nativities, whether Mars be in any of the Angles of the Figure, especially in Fixed Signs; or when Scorpio ascends, for then he destroys all the good signified by that question, or at least much impedes and diminishes it; unless Jupiter behold

him with a Trine or Sextile; for then his malice is mitigated; but yet as Jupiter is either strong or weak.

92. THE 92D is to observe in Nativities and Questions especially of death, whether the Lord of the House of Death, or Significator of death, Lord of the House in which the Lord of the Eighth is posited, applies to the Significator of the Native or Querent, or he to them, because a Planet so affected becomes the destroyer of Life, and kills as well if it be a Fortune as an Infortune, and that whether there be a Reception or not.

93. THE 93D is to consider if the Question concerns a thing that one would desire of another, or that one would get out of a secret hidden place, whether the Significator of the Querent, or thing inquired after, behold Saturn or is corporally joined to him; or whether Saturn be in the house of the thing inquired after, for then the business will hardly be done, or not without much labor and trouble, and mere tediousness than the Querent can imagine.

94. THE 94TH is to consider Questions. etc., whether the Significator of the thing inquired about be Cadent from the Ascendant, or other Angles, or from the house that signifies the thing or business sought after, or its Lord, or whether he be Retrograde, or in a bad condition with the Sun; or whether there be in the said house, signifying the thing inquired after, a Planet Cadent, or Retrograde, or in such ill condition with the Sun, or in an ill place from him, or ill aspected by him; for any of these things signify a hindrance to the thing, although otherwise the Question seems good and probable.

95. THE 95TH is whether the Planets signifying the thing sought, join mutually with each other; for that signifies it will be done; yet, be not too confident to judge so, till thou hast

well weighed the nature of the sign wherein they are joined, whether it be of their own nature; for then it will be easy, otherwise difficult; or scarce at all.

96. THE 96TH is to consider in Questions which seem to show, that what is enquired after shall be perfected, whether the Significator of the thing, and the Moon are in Angles; for if they both be above 25 degrees from Angles, it will not be accomplished; but if one shall and the other shall not be so far off, then it may be done but with difficulty, unless it be a journey; which will speed well enough if the significator be remote from Angles.

97. THE 97TH is to consider in what climate thou receives the Question; for judgment must be varied as the ascensions of countries and climates differ, there being not the order in the ascensions or elevations of signs, in one climate as in another, nor the same Ascendant in one region as in another.

Note by Lilly—"Beware therefore of a mistake here, for it will be very unhandsome and blameworthy; for whatever part thou travellest towards, from one region to another, whether from the East to the West, from the North to the South, or contrarily, your Ascendant will be changed from one degree from East to West in Longitude and e contra, and from the North to South, and the contrary. But some jocund fools or monks, in their cups, may arise and say, if your judgments are changed according to the situation of Nations they are false. But there is no talking to such brutes; they neither understand nor believe, nor is anything probable to them. Yet there are some very learned men amongst them, such as Conradus Brixiensis, a preaching Friar, who excellently understands Art and practiseth it honestly. Want of heeding what I have said hath made Astrologers to err, and I doubt doth so still, for right judgments cannot be given but by the Ascendant and other Houses, and therefore, if these vary, those must do so too. Therefore you should have Tables of Elevation for every Climate and Region; yet 'tis more difficult to find out the difference of one climate from another, than of one Region or country from another, according to the Longitude; for if thou hast tables of the elevation of the signs in any region from East to West, thou mayest by guess find the elevation in another, which way thou pleasest, either towards the East or West, according to the same climate, by taking the difference, but in diverse climate thou canest not so easily conjecture."

98. THE 98TH is to observe whether if what appears by the sign likely to be effected, be signified by the planets by corporal conjunction, or aspect or translation of Light, if by either of the two first the thing will be effected by the Querent, and the party enquired of, without any third person intermeddling; but if by the last it shall be done by ambassadors, friends, or some person interposing himself; and it shall be brought to pass by a person or thing signified by that House whose Lords translate the lights as aforesaid. Thus if it be the Lord of the second, it will be done by expenses, or a piece of money; if by the third, by some brother or the like; if by the fourth, by the Father, etc., according to the respective signification of each House.

99. THE 99TH is to consider well in Questions, Nativities, etc. what will certainly come of them; for sometimes by the Figure, a thing seems likely to be absolutely done; but is not wholly, but in part; sometimes it is wholly perfected, and sometimes neither wholly nor in part, upon which account astrologers are often blamed, and scarce know how to excuse

themselves, not knowing how this comes to pass, being a difficult point, and of a most subtle disquisition; so that the ancients would not meddle with it, save only the most honored Albumazar said something more than the rest, whose judgments I have found mere efficacious and correct than others, though Ptolemy, the great explainer of this science, must be acknowledged more curious than the rest. Now that which I say is the consideration of certain Fixed Stars.

Note by Coley—"Note that these fixed stars are now removed many degrees forwards in the Ecliptic than they were in the time of Bonatus, in respect of Longitude, which ought to be carefully considered by the industrious Astrologer, which I shall name, whereof some are of the nature of the Fortunes, and perfect those things with them not like to be perfected by the significations of the Planets; others are of the nature of the Infortunes, which suffer not things to be perfected according to the Planets significations, of which latter there are some in every sign, as in Bonatus' time there were two in the Head of Aries that is one, in 13°45', the other in 14°45', and are southern, and of the nature of Saturn and Mars. In Taurus are six stars, the first is 9°55', the Pleiades, which yet are called and counted but as one, and are of the nature of Mars and the Moon; another in 13°02', another in 14°45', called the Devil, another in 15°, called the Devil's Edad; another in the belly of Taurus, 19°15', called Aldebaran, which are all of the nature of Mars and Mercury. In Gemini there is one in 8°, called the Shoulder of the Dog, of the nature of Mars and Saturn; another in 10°15' of the nature of Mars, called the Warrior; another in 17°15'; another in 18°52', called the Witch, of the nature of the Sun and Mars. In Cancer, there is one in 2°03', called the Camel, of the nature of Saturn and the Moon; another in 7°55'; another in 13°, called the Western Camel, of the nature of the Sun and Moon; another in the same degree, called the Foot of the Dog, of the nature of Saturn, and another in 17°55' of the same nature. In Leo there is one in 15°55', of the nature of Saturn. In Virgo, two, one in 7°11', of the nature of Mars, the other in 15°, of the nature of Saturn. In Libra, one in 36°, of the nature of Saturn. In Scorpio, three, one in 1°03, another in 8°07', another in 9°, all of the nature of Mars. In Sagittarius, two small ones, one in 19°02', the other in 21°02', of the nature of Saturn. In Capricorn, two, one in 27°02', the other in 29°05', both of the nature of Saturn. In Aquarius, one in 9°04', of the nature of Mars and Saturn. In Pisces, one in 4°07' of the nature of Mars and Mercury.

"All these stars are hurtful and malevolent, hindering and destroying things after they seem probable to be accomplished, and therefore to be avoided as much as possible. Here it will not be superfluous but very convenient to insert a table of the fixed stars that have small latitude, as they are new placed, or rectify them for some succeeding years."[8]

100. THE 100TH consideration to observe the Fixed Stars

---

[8] This table is inserted at the end of the book. It must be born in mind that the fixed stars increase in longitude at the annual rate of 50.25" but their latitudes vary very little. The right ascensions and declinations of all the fixed stars mentioned in the two foregoing considerations, together with many others, are given every year in the Nautical Almanac, so that their places can easily be computed by means of their known annual differences, for past years and for many years in advance if necessary. There is an excellent article on the fixed stars in Wilson's *Dictionary of Astrology*, together with a table of all stars which are worthy of consideration in both Horary and Genethliacal Astrology. A useful table of the fixed stars will be found in *The Text-Book of Astrology*, Vol. 1, Genethlialogy, by Alfred J. Pearce (London, 1878). They are computed for January 1, 1876.

assisting and promoting the accomplishment of things, which are thus situated. In Aries there are two, one in 5°06', of the nature of Jupiter and Venus, another in 26°01', of the nature of Jupiter. In Taurus, three, one in the 1°03', another in 8°07', and the last in 9°0l', all of the nature of Venus. In Gemini are two stars, one In 19°02, the other in 21°08', both of the nature of Jupiter and of the second magnitude. In Cancer, likewise two, one to 2°02', the other in 29°05', both of the nature of Jupiter. In Leo, one in 9°04', of the nature of Jupiter and Venus. In Virgo, one in 4°07', of the nature of Jupiter and the Moon. In Libra, two, both cf the nature of Jupiter and Venus, one in 13°45', the other in l4°45. In Scorpio, four, one in 9°55', another in 13°01', a third in 14°45', the last in 19°l5', all of the nature of Jupiter. In Sagittarius, two, one in l0°15', the other in 7°55', both of the nature of Jupiter. In Capricorn, three, one 2°03', another in 7°55, both of the nature of Jupiter. In Pisces, two, one in 7°11' of the nature of Venus, the other in l4°59', of the nature of Jupiter. Wherefore always when thou findest the signification in a corporal conjunction with any of these, thou mayest pronounce happiness and a good end.

101. THE 101ST consideration is to mark in Nativities or Questions which Planet is the cutter-off of life or years, or hinderer of a thing from being done; for he it is who destroys the life of the Native, etc., who is strongest in testimonies of dignities or power, Yet Messabala concealed this, and discovered the secret only to a certain scholar of his, who out of pride appropriated the same to himself. Now after thou hast found who is this destroyer, etc., then see to whom the Lord of the Ascendant or the Moon is joined (who participates in signification of everything, as we have said before), or the Lord of the thing enquired after, and Lord of

the house of the Moon, or one or more of them; for if it be joined to a planet Retrograde or Combust, or Cadent from the Ascendant, or any other Angle, or to any of the Infortunes who doth not receive him, or is afflicted by an Infortune, which cuts off the light of the significator, the thing is destroyed, and so the years of the Native are diminished and he lives not long. Further, if the Lord of the Ascendant, or the Moon, or the Lord of the thing enquired after, be joined to a Planet who is free from the conjunction of the Infortunes, and so is safe as to himself but is joined to another Planet afflicted, some of the aforesaid ways, the matter shall be brought to nought, even after it seems accomplished, and the Native's life shall be suddenly cut off, when there is all the probability that may be of the contrary; and this will also happen though there be no conjunction with the killing Planet, if only the significator or Moon be afflicted in manner aforesaid.

102. THE 102D consideration is of things signified, how they shall be found or known, and from what significator they are to be taken, which must be from the significators of the Querent, and of the thing Questioned or enquired after; which two significators, if they shall be joined together with the Moon it signifies wholly and absolutely the effect of the thing; if not joined, then the contrary. And from the conjunction of the significators we ought to know why, or by what the question is made. And by the Lord of the House in which such conjunction happens, we know cf what the question will be, or the end thereof; for if that be a Fortune it will be good, according to the condition and signification of such Fortune, and the House wherein he is, and signification of the Lord of that House, and of the place in which the Lord is posited of that House wherein itself is. But if it be an

Infortune, it will be bad, according to the signification of the Infortune, and such other positions as aforesaid. If the Lord of the House or Exaltation, or of any two smaller Dignities, casts an aspect, or there be a translation of Light, you may know by that the question shall be brought to pass; but if there be none of these it cannot be precisely known, but it will be by or from a cause not yet discovered; and by the aspects of the Fortunes or Infortunes may be known what will be the effects.

103. THE 103D consideration is to mind in Nativities and general Questions in what House the Part of Fortune happens; for from the things signified by that House will the Fortune or gain of the Native or Querent arise, if the same be well disposed, otherwise the same will be cause of his misfortune and loss.[9]

104. THE 104TH consideration is to observe in Nativities and general Questions whether the significator of the Native or Querent be posited in the Seventh from his own House, or in Opposition to the Lord of the Ascendant; for he will not in such case signify gain from the things signified by that House, but rather expense and loss.

105. THE 105TH consideration is to observe in Nativities or general Questions, whether that an Infortune, unfortunate be in the Seventh, for that signifies that the Native or Querent shall not live in peace or any delight with his wives, sweethearts, or companions, but will perpetually have brawls and quarrels with them; it seldom happens otherwise from such a

---

[9] Wilson and most modern Astrologers do not regard the Part of Fortune in Nativities. In Horary Astrology, however, it has been proved very worthy of consideration.

position.[10]

106. THE 106TH consideration is to consider in Nativities and general Questions if a Fortune fortunate and in no way afflicted be in the seventh, for then the Native or Querent shall be happy in good wives and associates, yet shall have many rivals and persons that hate him, but rather out of envy than cause, so that he shall seldom bring his enterprises and designs to pass without much labor and trouble.

107. THE 107TH is to consider in Nativities and general Questions whether Mars be in the Second or in the Tenth and well disposed; for it denotes that the Native or Querent shall gain a Fortune or Estate by those persons that deal or work in Iron and Fire, as Smiths, Furnacemen, Glassmen, etc.; or in Victualing or keeping Inns, Taverns, etc.; but if Mars be weak or afflicted, loss and damage from all these.[11]

108. THE 108TH is to consider if neither of the Planets beholds two Houses, for his virtue and fortitude shall be in that wherein he hath most dignities, and which is most proper for him, and the thing he signifies.

109. THE 109TH is to consider whether the Lord of the Fifth be in the Seventh afflicted, for then the Native will never be happy at Feasts or Banquets; either be averse from

---

[10] In horary questions, should the Querent be unmarried, an Infortune in the Seventh House would then of course affect him through or by means of his open enemies, partners, or other matters or things ruled by that house.

[11] James Wilson, author of Dictionary of Astrology, and many others are of opinion that under any circumstances an Infortune in the second house is undesirable in a Genethliacal figure.

or slighted at such meetings, or some affront put upon him; nor will he ever go neat in his clothes, nor get any credit by them.

110. THE 110TH is to consider in Nativities whether Scorpio ascends, for such a Native is never like to get any great preferment in the Roman Church because Cancer (the Exaltation of Clerks (priests, parsons, etc.), will then be in the Ninth House, which signifies the Church, and Jupiter is an enemy to Mars, who is Lord of the Ascendant.

111. THE 111TH is to consider in Nativities and Questions especially of Law suits and controversies, whether the Dragon's Tail be in the Seventh, for that signifies damage or overthrow to the Native's enemies and prosperity to the Native or Querent, because the Dragon's Head will then be in the Ascendant. If it be in the Eighth it denotes the decay and loss of their estate or substance, and increase of the Native's. In the third, prejudice to the Native's brethren. In the fourth, to his Parents. In the fifth, to his Children. In the sixth, to his servants. In the ninth, to his journeys. In the tenth, to his preferment. In the eleventh, to his Friends. In the twelfth, to his cattle of the greatest sort, etc., and so to all other things signified by each House respectively; so do Saturn, and Mars also, but not so much. Likewise 'tis observable that other ill petitions may make void the said significations, but not so much as Saturn and Mars, unless they themselves are significators of the mischief, and then much of their malice is abated.

112. THE 112TH is strictly to examine and regard in every Nativity or Question, the Ascendant; for whosoever shall have Virgo ascend and Mercury in good condition, or at least not afflicted; if he study and practice Physic he shall have success and do great cures, but shall be unhappy in his salary

or profit thereby, not being able to get his fees of most of his Patients; and besides, shall be unhappy in Law suits. But if he follow the Law, he shall be unfortunate in all his business, and slighted; his words, though never so prudent, not regarded, no not by them for whose advantage he speaks, but a fool's discourse preferred, and whatever he meddles in shall turn out untoward, and people be his enemies without cause, and asperse and scandalize him, but they know not why. But far otherwise will it be if Sagittarius, Taurus, or Pisces ascend, and Jupiter, Venus and Mercury shall be in the Ascendant, or if Jupiter and Venus shall happen to be in Zaminium, or the heart of the Sun, whatever the Ascendant be the native shall be admired as a Prophet, and all his words received as Oracles, or the dictates of destiny.

113. THE 113TH is to consider whether either of the Infortunes be in the Ninth House, and without Dignity, for then the Native or Querent shall be often blamed and accused, and that without cause, as much as for one. But if a Fortune be there well affected (especially having Dignity there) he shall on the other side be praised, applauded, and honored, whether there be cause or reason for it or no.

114. THE 114TH is to consider whether the Lord of the Eighth be a Fortune, and in the Second, for then the Native or Querent shall gain considerably by the goods of people deceased, of his enemies, and by his wives, especially if such planet shall be free from impediment or have Dignities there. But if an Infortune be there, it signifies loss and decay of the Native's estate, unless he have dignities there and be otherwise well affected, and in good condition, for then it will be little or no prejudice; but without dignities, and in an ill state, it wholly and totally destroys and ruins all hopes of

estate.

115. THE 115TH is to consider whether the Eighth House or its Lord be afflicted, for then shall the Querent or Native be damnified, and lose an estate by the death of a wife, which she enjoyed for life or the like.

116. THE 116TH is to consider which of the Houses, or their Lords are afflicted, or under Impediment, for that signifies that hurt and damage will accrue to the Native, by reason of the things signified by that House and so on the contrary, it they are Fortunes, good and advantage from the same things.

117. THE 117TH is to consider if the Dragon's Tail be in the Fourth; for that signifies, that whatever the Native or Querent shall get shall be squandered away, and come to nothing; and wherever it is, it signifies damage to the Native in and from that House represented.

118. THE 118TH is to consider in what House a Fortune shall be fortunate and strong, well disposed, and not afflicted; for in and by these persons or things by that House signified, shall the Native or Querent gain profit, and make his fortune; and so on the contrary of a House that is afflicted.

119. THE 119TH is to consider if the Lord of the Second be in the Seventh, and the Seventh be in Aries, Scorpio, Capricorn or Aquarius; for then the Native's enemies shall easily take away his goods and right; and if he associate himself with persons, they shall rob him; and his wife or mistress shall cheat him, and steal whatever she can from him; unless the Lord of the Ascendant be in Trine or Sextile to the Lord of the Seventh, or in other aspects with reception.

120. THE 120TH consideration is to observe whether the Lords of any of these Eight Houses, viz., the third, fourth, fifth, sixth, ninth, tenth, eleventh, or twelfth, be in the Seventh, for whichsoever of them is there, the person by him signified will prove the Native's enemy, unless a perfect reception, with some good aspect as Trine or Sextile intervene. Yet a Square or Opposition with Reception will abate the enmity, but not wholly prevent it. Thus if it be the Lord of the Third, his Brethren will prove his enemies; if the Fourth, his Parents; if of the fifth, his Children, etc.; nor shall he gain of or by them so much as he shall lose another time; or if any of them sometimes appear kindly, it will be but from the teeth outward, and for their own ends, etc.

121. THE 121ST is whether the Moon be in the Eighth and the Lord of the Ascendant in the Ascendant, second, or twelfth, retrograde, for then the Native or Querent will not be Fortunate, nor have any luck at playing at dice or any other gaming.

122. THE 122D is whether the Part of Fortune be in the first 10 degrees of the Fourth House, with the Dragon's Head, the Moon, Venus and Jupiter, and they direct, for that signifies that the Native shall be lucky in discovering and finding out hidden treasure. If it be in the Second 10 degrees, or but with two of the said Planets, he shall find some, but not in so great quantity. In the last 10 degrees, and without one less, and yet a considerable parcel; and if only the Part of Fortune be there not afflicted, then a small quantity. If the Sun behold it with a Trine or Sextile, it will be Gold uncoined; if the Moon, silver; if Jupiter, a mixture of Gold and Silver, etc. If Venus, precious stones, Lockets, and for the most part Women's Ornaments. But if they be Retrograde, he shall dis-

cover the treasure, but not for himself; another shall get the profit. If the Lord of the Eighth behold the Lord of the Ascendant with a Square or Opposition, the finder shall die by reason of it; but if it be with a Trine or Sextile, he shall only catch some small disease or sickness. If the Dragon's Tail be there instead of the Head, he shall find it, but it shall be taken from him; or being ignorant what it is, he shall give it away almost for nothing; and if the Moon be then separated from the Lord of the Ascendant and joined to an Infortune that afflicts her, he to whom 'tis so given shall have little profit by it. If Mars or the Lord of the Eighth behold the Lord of the Ascendant, they that take it from him shall kill him. But if Mars and Saturn shall be in the place of Jupiter and Venus, the business will be only brass or copper or lead, and if the Lord of the Ascendant be with them, the discoverer is wearied with it, whatever it be, whether vile or precious.

123. THE 123D consideration is to observe in Nativities or questions whether the Sun and Moon are in Conjunction in one and the same minute, both according to Longitude and Latitude, and any of the Fortunes in the Ascendant, that is within 15 minutes above the cusp thereof, or 21 minutes below it; for that signifies that the Native shall be happy in getting a great estate and heaping up of money; but if they be only in exact Conjunction to Longitude, and not according to Latitude, and their distance one from the other be within 15 minutes, he will still be fortunate in acquiring substance; but so much the less by how much the further such distance is, and so proportionately. It they happen to be above 15 minutes distance, the same thou mayest conclude if the Moon shall be in the very minute of opposition to the Sun, and a Fortune be in the Seventh, which signifies the estate of the Querent or Native in respect of his wives, companions, or enemies. And

if at that time of birth Taurus ascend, and the Moon be there, or the very minute ascending, or Leo ascending, and the Sun in the minute ascending, and not afflicted by either of the Infortunes, it signifies that the Native shall get much money, and come to great preferment and honor; but it either of the Infortunes be in the said places instead of a Fortune, it denotes loss and destruction of estate to the Native or Querent by or on the occasions aforesaid.

124. THE 124TH consideration is to regard in Nativities and Questions, the Significators of the Querent's and Native's estate and also of his preferment, calling or profession; which thou mayest take to be the Lord of the Tenth, or of the Ascendant, if the other shall not be fit to signify the same; for if the Lord or Almuten of the Tenth be with the Light of Time or erect end tall from it, and distant 60 degrees or upwards even to 90 degrees, if it be one of the Superiors, or 30 degrees if it be one of the Inferiors, and in the Angle of the Tenth, or in the Ascendant within 30 minutes above the cusp, or a degree and a half below it, and not afflicted, it signifies that the Native shall attain to the Dignity and profession of his Ancestors, and not exceed it, yet shall be mere skillful, excellent, and perfect therein than any of them; but if there be in either of the said Angles any of the aforesaid helping and fortunate Fixed Stars with the Planet of Fortune or any of the Planets, he will far surpass his forefathers in dignity. And if such Fixed Stars shall be of the first Magnitude and sole Significators, the Native or Querent shall be raised to cast honors and riches, almost inestimable, which if beheld by the Lord of the Ascendant, then his fame and honor lies in his own Person; if by the Lord of the second, in his riches; if by the Lord of the Tenth, in his offices, command, or empire; and this though in never so poor and vile people; the meaner

their condition was, to so much the greater height shall they arrive. But this shall not endure long, for they seldom go beyond 27 or 30 years. And look, how much the more sublime was their fortune, by so much the more grievous, miserable, and calamitous shall be their fall, for they shall die an ignoble filthy death, or if they escape it, the same shall happen to their next successor.

125. THE 125TH consideration is to observe in Nativities or Questions what sign ascends; if it be the sign of a Planet that hath two Houses, the exercise or troubles of the Native or Querent shall be chiefly in those things signified by the other House of the said Planet, which shall lightly happen to him and for the most part through his own means. As if the Ascendant be in Aries, he shall be excused in those things as shall be the cause of his own death or fall because Scorpio, the other House of Mars, will be then in the Eighth House; but if Mars be well disposed and the Part of Fortune happen in the Eighth, he shall be very fortunate in all things signified by that House. If Taurus ascend, he shall be exercised in those things as shall cause his own weakness, because Libra, which is the other House of Venus, will be then the Sixth House. But if Venus be well disposed, and Part of Fortune in the Sixth, he shall be most lucky in things pertaining to the Sixth House. If the Ascendant be in Gemini, he shall be exercised in such things as shall occasion his being taken because Virgo, Mercury's other House, will be on the fourth; but if Mercury be well disposed and Part of Fortune in the fourth, he will be prosperous in things belonging to the Fourth House. If Virgo ascend, he will be exercised in things that will gain him honor and power, because Gemini, Mercury's other House, is in the tenth. If Mercury be then in Conjunction with the Part of Fortune and in the Ascendant,

he shall acquire, as it were, a King's revenue. But if Mercury be in the Tenth with the Part of Empire, fortunate and strong, he shall undoubtedly obtain a Kingdom or supreme command; and if this Part of Fortune and the Moon be also in the Tenth, he will be a mighty Prince infallibly. If Libra ascend, he shall be exercised in things that shall hasten his own death because Taurus, the other House of Venus, will be then in the Eighth. But if Venus be well disposed and the Part of Fortune in the Eighth, he will be lucky in things represented by the Eighth House, and so of any other sign. Scorpio ascending the Native or Querent shall bring diseases on himself because Aries is the Sixth. Sagittarius ascending, he shall fool himself into captivity because Pisces is on the Fourth. Capricorn ascending, he shall gain much by his industry, for Aquarius is then on the Second House. But if Saturn be ill disposed he shall squander away and waste his own substance idly. If Aquarius ascend, be shall procure himself many secret enemies, because Capricorn will be then in the Twelfth House. If Pisces ascend, he shall raise himself to honor.

126. THE 126TH consideration is to take notice in Nativities and Questions whether Mercury be significator wholly or in part, fortunate and strong, and in Capricorn or Aquarius, for then the Native shall be of profound and piercing wit, great understanding, and one that shall dive into the bottom of things, and see from the beginning what the issue will be; and so much the more if Saturn fortunate shall behold Mercury with a good aspect, especially if Mercury be in Aquarius, which is the delight of Saturn; and still more if a Fortune shall be with Mercury, and he with one of the propitious Fixed Stars. But if Mercury be in Aries or Scorpio, the Native will be bold, perfidious, inconstant, arrogant, and yet quick

of apprehension; rather nimble to repeat or find out things said by others than invent them himself.

127. THE 127TH consideration is to observe in Nativities if the Lord of the Ascendant be Saturn or Mars, and sole Lord of the Nativity, without any Fortune partaking in the dominion, the taste or smelling of the native or his complexion shall not be like those of other men, for if it be Saturn he shall delight in sour or insipid things, as Ralion Otolemy avers; if it be Mars, in sharp and bitter, flesh half stinking, wine dead, and pallid aloes, snuffs of candles, dung, etc., as also with filthy, dirty, unhandsome women; more than in others; or if it be a woman, in the homeliest men, etc.

128. THE 128TH consideration is in Nativities, whether the Ascendant be a human sign or the Lord of it in a human sign, for that signifies the native, an honest, sociable, and neighborly man, more especially if both happen together. But if the Ascendant carry the similitude of some creatures which men use to labor with, as Aries, Taurus, the last part of Sagittarius and Capricorn, the Native is very submissive and humble to men, yet very sociable. But if it be a sign half-feral, as Cancer and Pisces, he will be yet less sociable; but if it be feral, furious or salvane sign, as Leo and Scorpio, he will be of a brutish temper, delighting in the woods, hunting and living upon spoils and rapine; caring not to associate himself with men, so that he seldom remains long with his own Parents or nearest Relations.

129. THE 129TH consideration is to observe in Nativities whether the Moon be in Opposition to the Sun, with any of the stars called cloudy, which are Althazaic, and the Head of Gemini, or in a place called The Place of Falling into the Water, which Aquarius spouts forth, or the drops of the Lion,

said to be near his heart, and others which by reason of their mixture with each other do not shine distinctly (nebulous stars). For when the Moon shall not be above 10 minutes distance from them, according to Longitude and Latitude, it seems unavoidable that the native shall have diseases in his eyes not to be remedied by any human help or medicine. If the Moon be then Occidental in an Angle and Mars and Saturn likewise Occidental, not far distant from her, or opposing the Sun in any of the Angles, it signifies that the native shall be blind of both eyes at his death; nor does there appear any way whereby it may be prevented; but if it be not of luminaries, but only one, he shall lose but one eye, and if it be Sol and a man the right eye, if a woman the left eye; but if it be the Moon and a man, the left eye; but if a woman, the right eye.

130. THE 130TH consideration is to regard in Nativities whether the Moon be joined with Mercury by Body or Aspect, or there be a translation of light by any planet between them; if there be nothing of this and the sign ascending be neither of the nature of Mercury or the Moon, and Saturn in a diurnal nativity and Mars in a nocturnal, and one be in an Angle, the native will be mad, distracted, troubled with fits, a fool or at least exceeding forgetful unless a Fortune very strong shall at the sane time behold the Ascendant, Mercury, or the Moon; and so much the worse if the Angle wherein such Infortune is, happen to be Cancer, which is the exaltation of Jupiter, or Virgo, the exaltation of Mercury, or Pisces, the exaltation of Venus. The reason is because the Moon in Nativities is the general Significatrix of the native's Person, and the Planet with whom she is joined of his faculties and powers; and therefore if she be corporally joined or applying to such Planet, the native will prove of good understanding and very well retain his senses and intellectuals. And if Mer-

cury be in Capricorn or Aquarius, not afflicted, but in good condition, the native will be of an exceeding wit, and a great Philosopher, and if Jupiter and Venus be in Zamini Solis he will prove a Hermit or kind of Prophet whose words shall be received as Oracles beyond those of other men.

131. THE 131ST consideration is to take notice of the Nativity of a man, whether the Sun and Moon be both in Masculine Signs, or both in one Masculine Quarter or one Masculine sign, for if so, it signifies that the native's acts and temper shall be naturally such as belong to men. But in a woman's Nativity, the Luminaries so disposed make a kind of Virago, one that shall despise men, and obtrude herself into their affairs; and such a one, if she marry, will be sure to wear the breeches. If Venus and Mars shall be both in Masculine signs, the native will be moderately affected toward the delights of Venus, and use them according to nature and law; but if they happen to be Oriental, he will be more fallacious and immoderate, inclinable to incest, sodomy, etc. But if they be Occidental and in Feminine Signs, his spirits will be nasty and brutish; and so much the more if Saturn cast any Aspect to them. But if it be a Woman, and Mars and Venus Oriental and in Masculine Signs, she will abhor men's embraces and take no delight therein, but rather please herself with some little wantonness with persons of her own sex. But if Mars and Venus be in Feminine Signs and Occidental, she will love and take delight in men's kindness. And Ptolemy in his *Centiloquium* affirms that if Venus be joined with Saturn in a Nativity, and have Dignities in the Seventh, the Native shall be somewhat faulty and untoward in his venereal caresses.

132. THE 132D is to mark in nativities whether Man be corporally joined with a certain Fiery star of his own nature

in Taurus, called Algol[12], so that they are not above 16 minutes asunder, Mars applying thereunto and the Lord of the House wherein the Luminary, for the time ruling is pointed, which is called the Lord Anaubae; or of its Exaltation, and two others of its Dignities, and shall be in Opposition or Square of Mars, and neither of the Fortunes shall behold the Ascendant, nor be pointed in the Eighth House; it undoubtedly signifies the native shall be beheaded. And if Mars shall not be distant from it in Latitude above 6 minutes, it will infallibly happen so; not to be avoided but by God alone. And though a Fortune, Retrograde, or Combust should behold the Ascendant, yet it will scarce preserve him from beheading; only in such case it may happen not to be occasioned by his own fault, for a Fortune in such a case net impedited may save him from such an ill death, and permit him to die in his bed, but then it will be of some capital disease, proceeding from a hot house, and this before he comes to be fifty years of age. But if Mars shall not be thus affected, yet if an Infortune be in the Eighth, the Native shall come to an untimely or ignominious end; but if a Fortune be there in good state, he shall expire naturally; but if such a Fortune be afflicted, he shall die of some mischance coming upon him.

Note by Lilly—"Ptolemy, in his *Centiloquim*, tells us "that if the Light of the Time shall happen to be in the Mid-heaven (I say in the conditions aforesaid) such native shall be hanged! If either of the Infortunes be in Gemini, and the other in Pisces, his hands or feet shall be cut off, according to the signification of the sign wherein the Planet is pointed which is most malevolent. If Mars be in conjunction

---

[12] Caput Algol (*B Persei*), a star of the 2d magnitude, now in 24°17' of Taurus of the nature of Saturn and Jupiter. It is held to be the most unfortunate, vident and dangerous fixed star in the heavens.

with the Lord of the Ascendant in Leo, and hath no Dignities in the Ascendant, nor neither of the Fortunes in the Eighth, the native shall be burnt to death; and if Mars be then Retrograde, Combust, or in his Fall, it will be for some crime, otherwise by mischance or unjustly. Ptolemy saith that if Saturn, in a Nativity, be in the mid-heaven and the Planet to which he is Anauba (a Depositer) be in apposition to him, and a dry sign in the Cusp of the Fourth, the native shall be knocked on the head or die by some ruins falling on him; but if a moist sign be there, he shall be drowned; but if it be an human sign, he will be strangled. If Mars or Saturn be in the Ascendant at birth, and Peregrine, the native shall have a scar or mark on his head or face; if the Infortune be afflicted, Combust or Retrograde, the same will be very deformed, and much disfigure him, otherwise not."

133. THE 133D consideration is to mark in Nativities, whether Gemini or Sagittarius ascend, and whether its Lord be well disposed, that is, fortunate and strong, and likewise the Moon, for that signifies that if the native live, he will get great riches. If Virgo or Pisces ascend and its Lord or the Moon be well affected, he shall get money and lay the same out well, and live splendidly, being beloved for his generosity and bounty. But in the other case where the Ascendant is Gemini or Sagittarius, he will not be so liberal, but very frugal and sparing; besides, he who hath Gemini or Virgo for his Ascendant may lose his estate and come to want; but he that hath Sagittarius or Pisces shall never lose his means, nor fall into poverty. If Aries, Scorpio, Capricorn, or Aquarius ascend, the native will be miserably covetous. If Jupiter behold the Ascendant, he may somewhat mitigate the sordid humor, but will not wholly prevent or take it away.

134. THE 134TH is to mind in Nativities, whether Mars or Venus be in the Sixth, and likewise well disposed, for that signifies that the native shall be not really fit for Physic, and grow a perfect doctor in every part of the Art. If Mercury be in conjunction with Venus and she Retrograde, he will make naturally a good singer; but if Mercury be in the Twelfth not afflicted, he will be studious and famous in most sciences, especially Philosophy.

135. THE 135TH consideration is to consider in Nativities whether the Lord of the Ascendant and the Moon, and Jupiter, and Venus, are either all in the Ascendant, or whether Jupiter and Venus behold the Lord of the Ascendant, and the Moon in the Ascendant by a Trine or Sextile, and free from affliction, for then the native will prove very strong and courageous; and none will dare to disobey his commands.

136. THE 136TH consideration is to note in the Nativities of Kings and rich men, and such grandees as are fit to bear rule, whether both Luminaries are in the Degrees of their Exaltations, or in their own Houses, in the same degree one with the other, and free from affliction, for this signifies that the native shall obtain great honors; for he shall be made Emperor or something like it so that he shall be, as it were, monarch of the world, which shall continue to the fourth generation of his posterity. But if all the Planets below Jupiter shall be disposed of by him and he shall receive virtue from every one of them, notwithstanding the condition aforesaid, and afterwards commit both them and himself to Saturn, and both be Oriental from the Sun and in Angles, the native will be a person of great renown and power, although perhaps not with the title of king; but his fame shall endure for a long time, all his lifetime; and after his death for three revolutions of Saturn, or longer.

137. THE 137TH is to see whether Mercury be in conjunction with Saturn in the Ascendant, for that signifies that the native is a foolish talkative fellow that would be counted wise; he shall speak ill of both men and women; the greatest wit he hath is to invent many lies; nor doth he ever open his mouth, but something of untruth appears intermixed with his discourse, so natural it will be for him to tell lies, Saturn give him a foul tongue, and Mercury a sharpness of malice to employ it.

138. THE 138TH is to see in Nativities whether the two Infortunes are in the Fourth House, or whether the Angles are possessed with moveable signs, and Mars and Saturn in them, for then the native will be poor, wretched, and unfortunate above all others, all his lifetime, unless Jupiter or the Lord of the Triplicity ascending prevent.

139. THE 139TH is to be careful, both in Nativities and Questions, where the Dragon's Tail is, for that signifies the wasting and destruction of the thing signified by that House, and especially if it relate to gain; for in the first it signifies expenses and loss of gain to the Querent from or by reason of his person; in the Second, destruction and loss of money and substance; in the Third, loss by means of Brethren, Sisters, Neighbors, etc.; in the Fourth, damage that one shall sustain by one's Grandfather, Father-in-law and such things relating to Inheritances; and that the Native shall change Houses often, and get little by it; in the Fifth, damage from or by reason of children; in the Sixth, losses by servants or small cattle; in the seventh, loss by Women, Companions or open enemies; in the Ninth, loss by Religious Men, and on the account of Religion; to the Tenth, by or in his preferments, honors, etc.; in the Eleventh, loss by his Friends, or for their sakes; and in

the Twelfth, damage sustained by great Cattle, or by means of hidden enemies.

Editor's Note: The author left out the Eighth House. Modern Astrologers do not consider the effects of the Dragon's Head or Tail. If, however, they are worthy of consideration, the effect of the Dragon's Tail in the Seventh house would be to entail loss on the Native or Querent's wife's money or goods, etc.; it would also prejudice the money, goods, chattels, etc. of his partners, open enemies, and opponents in law suits, and would be generally unfavorable to such matters or things as are ruled by the eighth house, having due regard to other testimonies shown in the figure. It must be remembered that with the Dragon's Tail in the eighth house the Querent or native has the Dragon's Head in the second house (that of wealth) and therefore but little damage could accrue to the Querent or Native through loss of his or her actual personal money, goods, chattels, etc., according to this single testimony.

140. THE 140TH consideration is to see whether the Significator of the thing in question or the Moon be so weak that it cannot bring the matter to perfection, and if they be, take the Significator of the Querent and thing inquired after, and subtract the lesser from the greater, and add to the remainder the degrees of the sign Ascending, and project what they amount unto from the Ascendant, and observe where it happens; for the Lord of that sign signifies what was enquired of and according to his conditions shall thou give Judgment, as thou findest him fortunate and strong, or unfortunate and weak. For if the business concern a man's estate, and he be placed in the second, as he is, so shall the Querent's estate prove; if in the Third, the Brethren, Neighbors, etc.

will be disposed accordingly; in the Fourth, those of greatest Relations; in the Fifth, the Children; in the Sixth, Servants; in the Seventh, Wives; in the Eighth, Wives' portions; in the Ninth, long journeys; in the Tenth, his preferments; in the Eleventh, his Friends; in the Twelfth, his secret Enemies.

141. THE 141ST is to consider in Nativities the gifts and properties bestowed on men by the Fixed Stars, and how long they continue, together with the reason why they prove, not lasting as those which proceed from the Planets, since it seems a little probable that they should continue longer than those; of which I do not remember to have met with anything in the Ancients, save only that Ptolemy in his *Centiloquim* says the Fixed Stars sometimes confer exceeding great benefits; but oftentimes they end ill. And Almansa, in his Treatise to the Great King of the Saracens, says that the Fixed Stars bestow notable gifts, and raise from poverty to happiness and high degree more than any of the seven planets. Now the reason that the gifts of the Fixed Stars to men abide less with them than those given by the Planets is because the Fixed Stars being the Agents, and men the Patients, the subject on which they are to operate are not agreeable to them, nor are born to be able to receive their impression; for it is requisite that there should be some conformity and likeness, or agreeableness between the Agent and the Patient; but the Fixed Stars are most slow in motion and consequently in mutation, whence it comes to pass that their impressions require subjects and patients of the same nature; that is to say, such as are the most lasting, and carry a conformity with them to perfect or accomplish their effects. For the Revolution of the Fixed Stars is finished, but in six and thirty thousand years, but the Viventhipolis, or life of man, generally exceeds not three revolutions of Saturn; that is to say, the space of ninety years;

very few exceed that age, though possibly some may by the addition of the years of some Planets to the years of the Alcocoden in their Nativities, which bears no conformity or proportion with 36,000 years to complete the effects of their influences. And therefore as an Eagle cannot exercise the complement of her flight or power on a Fly, nor a Stone coming forth (*Sunda trabathi*) do any great execution (*in Musciovem*) no more can the Fixed Stars complete the effects of their impressions; and therefore their gifts or the good promised by them continue no longer with men because men are of so small a duration and subject to a swift mutability in respect of their Motion. And upon this is that Aphorism grounded, that Advises to make use of Fixed Stars in the foundation of Cities, but of Planets in the erection of Houses; because Cities are generally of the longest continuance amongst corruptible things, and far more durable than particular Houses; for these in respect of their individuals do not endure always, whereas Cities remain by a successive building and rebuilding of Houses; and therefore though Castles are very lasting, yet are they not equal to this respect to Cities; so that although he may use the superior planets in elections for building Castles, it is better to take Fixed Stars; yet still because Cities are of longer continuance than Castles, they are more appropriated to the Fixed Stars, whose Subjects they are, for the impression which a solid thing makes in a more solid thing, continues much longer than that which it makes on a less solid thing; and far less in a thing not solid, then a thing somewhat solid; and yet less in a very slippery transient thing than in a thing less lubricous or changeable. Hence the Impressions which the fixed Stars make on Cities are more correlative to them in length of time, and accordingly those of Castles ware durable than those of Houses, for the same reason proportionally. But bodies of men are more remote from those fixed stars than Houses themselves, and so more corruptible; and for that cause their Significations apply less to them, or if they happen, abide but little; the Significations of the Fixed Stars being so great and noble, so high and free from corruption and mutability, that they cannot easily take upon them a variable commixture with things quickly corruptible and suddenly changeable, unless it be as oil on water; for though it may enter into it, yet such impression will not long continue; for the fixed Lights operate with so much nobleness that by reason of their long distance from those vile corruptible changeable bodies, and neighborhood to the Supreme Light, their effects cannot remain in or with them when they are lightly or suddenly changed and corrupted; especially in base people and mean spirits, for they seldom transcend his person to whom they happen, and oftentimes leave him whilst he lives, and that to his damage, so great that God alone can prevent; as I affirm for the most part; though 'tis possible they may sometimes terminate in good and continue long, as it hath sometimes happened that some have lived to the greatest years of the Alcocogen, of whom I never saw but one in my time, who was named Richard, who affirmed himself to have been a Courtier under Charles the Great, King of France, and that he had lived 500 years. At what time there was a report of one that had continued alive ever since our Savior's days called Johan Buttadeus because he had said to the Lord as he was led to be crucified, Who said to him, "Thou shalt expect, or wait for me, till I come." The aforesaid Richard I saw at Ravenna in the year 1223, and the said John is said to have passed through Florilivium, in his Journey to St. James at Compostella in the year 1267. Nor could the Significations of the Fixed Stars be applied; or adhere to men nor sensibly remain in them, unless there were some Medium by which they might Act upon them which are the Planets, which are secondary Agents, as the first are principal; for whenever there are diverse actions in order, attributed to several Agents, the principal act ought to be referred to the principal Agent, which in respect of the effects on corruptible things was the Primary Cause. And the Planets are Secondary, for that corruption which those inferiors suffer happens by reason of their too great distance from the incorruptible superiors; yet their effects sometimes continue long in Grandees, and persons very rich, who are apt for Empire, magnanimous, and of brave and excellent spirits; such as in my time was the Emperor Frederick the Second who, when he was indigent and in great necessity, was arrived to the Imperial Dignity, and brought under his obedience all Apulia, the Kingdom of Sicily, Jerusalem, Crocovia, Italy and the whole Roman Empire (except Lombard) subduing all Enemies, Traitors and Rebels, and remained in that illustrious nourishing condition; yet at last died miserably, being poisoned by his domestics, and all his family extirpated so that scarce any of them remained. Such an other was Ecilinus de Romano, who when he was but mean, was far exalted above all other Italians, for he ruled and, as it were, tyrannized over the Marquisate of Treves even to Almaine and Trent, and within four or five miles of Venice, and his Tyranny continued twenty-six years; but at last all these glories were overcast with calamity, for when it seemed impossible to suppress him, he fell into the hands of his enemies at a battle in the Country of Mediolanensi apud Cassianum, and died wretched, and all his posterity was destroyed, not one of them remaining. In the same manner there was in the Kingdom of Apulias of base descent, called Peter de Vinea; who when he was a scholar at Bononia was forced to beg for his living, and had not bread to eat, yet was made a notary, and after that

Protonotary of the Court of the Emperor Frederick the Second, he became a Judge and climbed to such grandeur that he was happy that could obtain the least of his favor, for whatever he did the Emperor would confirm; but himself would often set aside what had been established by the Emperor, who made him Lord of Apulia, whereby he grew so rich that he had 10,000 pounds of Gold besides other Treasures almost inestimable; yet in the end he fell, and was reduced to such misery that the Emperor ordered his eyes be put out; enraged at which out of mere indignation he struck out his own brains against a wall, as it was then commonly reported. Another was at Pysa called Smerolus, one of the drefs of the vulgar who came to be, as it is said, Lord of that Province; nor durst any of the nobility for a while contend with him, yet at last he came to nothing. After whom one Oddo Gualduzius, a mean fellow, tapered up so high that he did as it were, sway the whole City and none would contradict him, till Galyver, a Judge, caused him to be chopped all to pieces. The same happened at Florylycium. One called Simon Mustaguere, the son of obscure Parents, who mounted so high that all the people adored him; no durst any oppose him, save only myself, who knew him thoroughly; and what mischief he could, he did at his pleasure for three years space, but at last down he came being banished from the City which happened tor the odiousness of his person and cowardice. Another being a Prior of the Preaching Order, by name John, by Nation Vicentinus, was admired as a Saint by all the Italians that acknowledged the Roman Church; but I ever thought him an Hypocrite; he grew so nigh that he was reported to have raised 18 from the Dead (though never one of them could be seen), and to cure all diseases, fright Devils, etc., yet could I not perceive anybody freed by him, though I made much enquiry into his miracles; however, the whole world seemed to run after him, and he thought himself happy that could get a thread of his Cap, which they esteemed equal with the relics of the Saints; and in his preaching he would publicly boast that he had Converse with Jesus Christ, the Virgin Mary, and Angels when he list. By which tricks, the Friars of his order at Bononia got more than 20,000 marks. And his power was so great that by his own will he released a soldier as he was going to Execution for Murder; nor durst the magistrates deny him, nor speak ill of him but myself, who knew all his wheadles and cozenages for which the rabble, merely out of fear of him, reported me an Heretic. In which esteem and pomp he continued above a year, but at last went out like the snuff of a candle, with a stink, his devices and hypocrisy being discovered, so that he became as generally, and everybody was ashamed to be seen in his company.

142. THE 142D consideration is to observe in Nativities and general questions the gifts and good advantages bestowed on men by the Planets; because those are applied more easily to them and continue longer extended to their successors, according as they are well disposed in the Radical of their Nativities; but they are seldom exceeding great, unless when applied by fortunate Fixed Stars; because being of a more swift mutability they have a closer affinity with them, especially if proceeding from the inferior Planets; for their conformity with men, their correlative subjects. These of the superiors last not so long with men but in building of houses they are much better than the other.

Note by Lilly—"Of the Good given by Saturn and Other Planets, Saturn Oriental and well disposed, that is strong and in Reception, gives great fortune in building, planting trees requiring a long growth, in manuring ground, erecting waterworks and the like. Jupiter gives good luck in Sciences such as the Law; and Dignities, being made a Bishop, a Judge, or the like. Mars in leading forth of Armies, etc., Sol in Lay Preferments, as Kingdoms, Governments, etc.

"But the lower Planets bestow their gifts inherent to men and more durable, as Venus in the attempts of women, their ornaments, courting them, etc. Mercury in trading, writing, etc. The Moon in navigation, planting vines, using drinks, selling wine, etc. All these I say are excellently well bestowed by the Planets advantageously posited, and endure longer, that is to say. The prosperities given by the Moon may continue to the seventh year or generation, because she is the seventh Planet reckoning downwards; and if they pass the seventh age or generation they cannot exceed the eighth as suppose from the 42d year to the 45th year including those of Mercury may endure to the sixth age, being the sixth from Saturn, but will scarce hold out the seventh. Those of Venus to the fifth age, she being the fifth Planet from Saturn; but will not exceed the sixth. Those of the Sun to the fourth age. Those of Mars to the third age. Those of Jupiter to the second age. Those of Saturn only for one age, and cannot transcend; nay seldom reach the third. And though I say they may continue so long, yet do I not say that they shall not be finished before, for as Aristotle says, there are terms that cannot be passed over; yet he does not say but that they may be prevented and come short off; so in these cases; and further, when I say that they cannot continue longer, I mean without vanishing wholly, or so depressed, that it will be no more like what was before, than green or russet to a perfect white unless by chance something from another cause happens anew; which seldom chances, nor can truly be said to be the same, but quite another thing from the first. Hence comes perhaps the common observation that goods or possessions ill got never abide to the fifth or third age; many that use that proverb not knowing whence it comes to pass but only because they have heard others say so or seen it often happen thus. But from what we have here laid down, some reason may be given; for ill gotten goods count such as are got by way of usury, lies, deceit, theft, rapine, and the like."

143. THE 143D consideration is to understand the true method of judging, and by what ways thou mayest come to some result, that thou mayest examine and rightfully discuss the same, and discover the truth of what the stars shall show thee. And herein there are 14 points to be considered and heeded:

1. Whether the Querent proposes the question really and intentively or not. For if the Lord of the Ascendant and Lord of the hour be the same or the Signs wherein those Significators are placed be of the same Triplicity or complection the Question is serious; but otherwise, if the Ascendant shall be the end of any Sign, the Question is not Radical.

2. Behold the Ascendant and his Lord, the Moon and the Planet from which she separates and assign them for Significators of the Querent; the Seventh and the Planet with which the Moon is joined, shall represent the person enquired after; but if it be necessary, descend to the persons, as the things are signified by the Houses, from the first to the twelfth.

3. Consider the nature of the thing enquired about, the House and Sign whereby it is signified.

4. The Aspects of the Planets both good and malevolent to the Significators of the things sought after.

5. In what place from its own House each of the Significators are, viz., whether in his own or the second, third, cr fourth, etc., or in the Combust way or the like places.

6. Whether they are found in Angles Cadent or Succedent Houses.

7. Diligently see where the Querent's Assistants must come, viz., whether from a Father, a Son, a King, a Kinsman, or a Friend, etc.

8. By the mirth of the Querent, as if the Lord of the Ascendant shall be in the fifth, or elsewhere joined with its Lord, free from being afflicted by the Infortunes. Or by his sadness, as if his Significator happen in the Sixth, Seventh, Eighth, or Twelfth, unless the question be of things signified by those Houses and as thou findest so Judge.

9. By the Fortunes and Infortunes, according as thou findest them in places signified, the things about which the Querent is moved; and if the benevolents are more, 'tis good, if otherwise the contrary; if the testimonies are equal, then indifferent.

10. Whether the Lord of the Ascendant be in the House of the thing enquired after, or with its Lord.

11. In what House the Lord of the first is joined with the Significator of the things looked after; for by the Significator of that House, or his occasion, thou mayest judge the matter will be brought about.

12. If the Significators are not joined there, whether there be any Translation of Light between them by any Planet, or receives their description, thou shalt judge the same thing.

13. By the natures of the Significators themselves, agreeing in their natures and significations with each other.

14. According as the receiver of the Significator's virtue or disposition shall be a Fortune or Infortune strong or weak, and does behold the Significator, or the Moon, or any with aspect of love or enmity, so shalt thou pronounce judgment.

144. THE 144TH consideration is to observe in Questions, Nativities, or Elections, when the Significators shall not clearly show thee what thou wouldest know but the signification remains dubious, so that the mind is in suspense, take the place of the Lord of the Ascendant, and the place of the Lord of the House of the Moon, and see the distance of degrees between them, beginning from Aries, of which make signs, and add the degree of the sign ascending; and project from the Ascendant as well by day as night, and where the number falls, the Lord of that House shall be Significator and from him take the signification of the business enquired, for according to his disposition thou mayest Judge.

145. THE 145TH consideration is that thou see in Diurnal Nativities, whether Cor Leonis[13] be in the Ascendant, that is to say in the Oriental Line or above it one degree or below it

---

[13] Regulus (*a Leonis*) a Star of the 1st magnitude in 28 degrees 8 minutes of Leo of the nature of Mars; it is said to give glory, wealth, and great honors, chiefly by military preferment; but the glory promised by such Stars as Aldebaran, Hercules, Bellatrix, Antares, etc., and all which are of the nature of Mars, is said to be transient.

three degrees; or whether it be in the Tenth in like degrees, without the Conjunction or Aspect of any of the Fortunes; for this alone signifies that the Native shall be a person of great note and power, too much exalted, and attain to high preferment and honors, although descended from the meanest parents. And if any of the Fortunes behold that place also, his glory shall be the more increased; but if the Nativity be nocturnal, his fortune will be somewhat meaner, but not much; but if the Infortunes cast their aspects there it will still be more mean; but if the Fortunes behold it also they will augment the good promised a fourth part, and mitigate the evil as much; yet still whatever of all this happens, it signifies that the Native shall die an unhappy death qr at least that all his honors, greatness, and power shall at last suffer an eclipse, and set in a cloud.

146. THE 146TH consideration is that thou take the place of the Lord of the Ascendant, and the place of the Lord of the Twelfth, and subtracting the lesser from the greater add to the remainder the degrees of the sign ascending and project from the Ascendant; and where the number falls the Lord of that sign shall be partner with the Lord of the Question and shall be called the Principal Partner. Again, take the place of the Lord of the said sign, and the place of the Lord of the Part of Fortune, and subtracting the lesser from the greater add the degrees of that sign ascending; and where the number falls, the Lord of the sign shall be another Partner, and be called the Secondary Partner; which if it happen to be the same Planet, regard only that; but if different, then take both and subtract the lesser from the greater and add the degrees of the sign ascending, and the planet on whose House the number falls shall be the third Partner; and which of those three is the strongest shall be the chiefest sharer in the significations of

the thing enquired after. If all the remainders, or two of them, shall happen in the House of one Planet, that shall be preferred. If the Question seems good, and those Partners are ill disposed, they will diminish of the good signified by the Question, and so on the contrary; but if the Question seem evil, and they are well disposed, they will allay and mitigate the evil signified by the Question, and so likewise on the contrary.

End of the Considerations of Guido Bonatus

Choice Aphorisms
from the
Seven Segments of Cardan

General Aphorisms

1. Life is short, Art long, Experience not easily obtained, Judgement difficult, and therefore it is necessary that a Student not only exercise himself in considering several Figures, but also that he diligently read the writings of others who have treated rationally of this Science, and make it his business to find out the true natural causes of things by experiments, to know the certain places and processions of the Planets and Fixed Stars, Constellations, etc., but above all to be a passionate layer of truth.

2. The Principles of Art are three: Reason, Sense, and Experience. But the Principles of Operations are four, viz.: The Planets, The Parts of Heaven, The Fixed Stars, and the

Site or Position[1] of all these in respect of one another.

3. There are some things perfectly known, as the Circle of Ascension; some in a competent measure, as the Revolution of the Sun; some may be known although they yet are not, as the Revolution of the Superiors; some things fall under knowledge, yet cannot be exactly known, as the precise Ingress of the Sun Into the Equinoctial point; some are neither known, nor can be known, as the complete commixtures and distinct virtues of the Stars.[2]

4. It Is much worse for an Artist to conceive be knows those things which he is ignorant of than to be ignorant of those things which he ought to know.

5. Mean learning with an excellent judgement avails more than a mean judgement with the greatest learning, yet is judgement very much assisted and perfected by learning; but everything prospers better, and is far more easily perfected that has nature for its guide and favorable stars, than that which is attempted by human industry though never so diligent.

6. He that has too great a conceit of himself will be apt to fall into many errors in his judgement; yet on the other side,

---

[1]Aspects and Configurations.

[2] Modern astrologers are now thoroughly acquainted with all but the complete commixtures and distinct virtues or powers of all the stars. Herschell and Neptune being unknown to the Ancients, were not considered by them, and at the present time, therefore, owing to the science having lain for many years dormant, so to speak, the influences of these two planets are not yet thoroughly understood. It is conceived by the best modern Astrologers that Herschell is of the nature of Saturn and Mars, and Neptune of the nature of Venus, though infinitely milder in influence.

he that is too diffident is not fit for this Science.

7. He that would truly promote Art must insist as much on the confutation of false opinions delivered by others, as in the declaration of truth.[3]

8. An Astrologer is so far only true and honest, as he depends in his conjectures on principles of natural philosophy,[4] and since those Arts which are inherent in their proper subjects cannot promise any certainty concerning matters to come, the Astrologer ought never to pronounce anything absolutely or peremptorily of future contingencies.

9. Truths of themselves are to be desired, for Science itself is a certain good, now the expectation of future good very much delights us, and on the contrary, when future evils are foreseen, we may either avoid them,[5] mitigate them, or at least bear them more contentedly.[6]

---

[3] Lilly and Partridge made a point of acting up to this Aphorism, as may easily be ascertained from a perusal of their works.

[4] Cardan here means that an Astrologer should base his judgments on the established and approved rules of Judicial Astrology, and not be too eager to form principles of his own with regard to judgments on any contingencies which may arise and which are not plainly shown in the Figure under consideration.

[5] The prudent man foreseeth the evil, and hideth himself.—Proverbs, c. 22, v. 3; c. 28, v. 12.

[6] "A skillful person acquainted with the nature of the stars is enabled to avert many of their effects, and to prepare himself for those effects before they arrive.

"A sagacious mind improves the operation of the heavens, as a skillful farmer by cultivation improves nature."—Claudius Ptolemy, *Tetrabiblos*, The Centiloquy.

10. Heaven is the instrument of the moat High God, whereby he acts upon and governs inferior things.

11. He that asserts things that can never be proved by experience is deceived and ambitious, but thus it always happens, those that are most ignorant of Art delight to boast of doing things difficult or wonderful.

12. It Is all one as to promoting of Art, etc., and the knowledge thereof, either from Nativities known, to predict what shall happen, or after accidents have happened, to discover the Nativities before unknown which are thereby rectified[7], but as to vulgar opinion, the first way far exceeds the last.

13. He that goes about to destroy Art is far worse than he that is unskilled in it, for his mind is full of malice and idleness as well as ignorance.

14. Men may be said almost to be compelled by the Stars, even in voluntary actions, by means of their corrupt affections and ignorance.

15. Always deliver judgements from the Stars in general

---

[7] This involves the doctrine of Rectification, i.e., the method of bringing a nativity to its true time, as it is supposed that the inaccuracy of a clock or watch, or the mistake of those whose business it is to observe them, may cause an error in the time of birth which requires to be rectified. Several methods a re recommended for this purpose, of which the oldest probably is the animondar of Ptolemy; we have the *Truitine* of Hermes, the methods of Argol, Morin, Kepler, etc. Placidus (De Titus, author of the *Primum Mobile*) is wholly silent on the subject of rectification. Not one of his thirty nativities are rectified, although he seems very much to doubt the correctness of some of them. The safest events to rectify a nativity are those of accident and marriage.

terms, or if thou dost otherwise let it be when thou hast very evident testimonies and in great and weighty matters.

16. We ought not to use arguments or tedious discourses in giving judgement, much less flatteries, but only to pronounce what is known by experience and firm reason.

17. A main reason why events are so rarely foretold by Astrologers is because the Art is yet but imperfectly discovered, for hitherto those that have been most excellent in it, being commonly old persons, have despaired to live to see the fortunes of children newly-born, and the Nativities of persons grown up, being uncertain, they scarce thought them worth so much labor.

18. When true genitures exactly taken in accidents prove false or absurd, and not agreeable to the things signified, they are to be accounted monstrous[8], and are to be avoided as anatomists do monstrous bodies in their dissections; for they overthrow Art.

19. Generals are to be gathered from Singulars, and Singulars from Generals, and an Artist ought always to learn to distinguish between that which is by itself, and that which is only by accident.

20. The strength and efficacy of Fixed Stars is to be considered from their magnitude, their splendors, their natures or properties, their nearness to the Ecliptic, their place in the World, their multitude, their first oriental appearance, the pu-

---

[8] The Planet Uranus, not known in Cardan's time, has doubtless much to do with showing monstrous births and also eccentricity of manner and life. His effects are not well understood, however, by modern Astrologers.

rity of their place, the similitude or agreement of the body or rays of a Planet with them and their circle of position.

21. The Light of the Time is the Sun in the day, and morning twilight; and the Moon in the night when she is above the Earth, and in her morning rising; so that sometimes there may be two Lights of Time, sometimes it so happens that there is none.

22. When a Planet is within five degrees of the cusp of any house, it shall be accounted to have virtue in that house though actually posited behind the cusp in another house.

23. Not only Trines and Sextiles may be counted friendly aspects, but even Squares and Oppositions too, if there happen a Reception.[9]

---

[9] This more especially is the case with the Fortunes, Jupiter and Venus, in Horary questions.

Aphorisms Relating to Nativities

1. A Child is then said to be born when first it breathes in air at its mouth, when outside its mother's womb.[1]

2. Those that have the Luminaries unfortunate in Angles will be apt to commit suicide.

3. Those that have Saturn in Opposition to Jupiter will never enjoy peace, and those that have the Dragon's Tail with Jupiter, will seldom be rich.

4. Those that have Saturn and Mars in the same part[2] of the Zodiac will be liable, in the course of their lives, to many misfortunes; and if they shall both be in Taurus, and posited in the fourth house, when the Ascendant, by direction comes to their rays, the Natives will have some severe falls, or be in danger by reason of some ruinous building falling on them.

5. Fixed Signs give learning, with the exception of Scorpio; Common Signs, manners and conversation, with the exception of Virgo; and Moveable Signs, riches, with the exception of Capricorn; whence it appears that those are bad Nativities that have all the Planets in Virgo, Scorpio or Capricorn.

6. If the Ascendant be one of those Signs called Mute,

---

[1] Wilson, in *Dictionary of Astrology*, says the nativity takes place the instant the Native draws breath (independently, or rather that when the umbilical cord is divided.

[2] In the same sign. Cardan probably meant Saturn and Mars in Conjunction.

and Mercury in one that is not humane, with any Fixed Star of the nature of Saturn, the Native will never speak well, but bring forth his words with difficulty.

7. He that hath the Moon in Taurus[3] in the second separating from the Square or Opposition of Jupiter, and applying to the Trine of the Sun shall obtain very considerable riches.

8. When the Abscissor, cutter off of life, or killing Planet[4], is on the Ecliptic, and an Infortune in an Angle, the Native will die a violent death.

9. When an Infortune is posited on the cusp of the seventh house, the Native will be liable to great calamities[5], and if an Infortune be in Aspect with the Sun or Moon afflicted in the same place, the Native, though a Prince, shall suffer a world of troubles.

10. Aries ascending signifies the Natives to be handsome and of a grave, composed temper, but Scorpio on the horoscope notes them to be great liars.

11. When the Moon is in Scorpio in Square of Saturn in Leo, or in Opposition to him when he is partially in Taurus, the Native rarely has either wife or children. If Saturn be in Aquarius, he will be a mere woman-hater.

12. If the Dragon's Tail be with Saturn in Square of the Moon, and she Cadent, the Native will be consumptive, espe-

---

[3] The Moon is exalted in 3° Taurus.

[4] Termed also the Anareta.

[5] He will seldom be fortunate in his married life.

cially if from an Angle; but if besides it be in Square to the Lord of the Ascendant, he will be sickly and infirm all the days of his life, and if such Aspect happen in or from the sixth house, so much the worse.[6]

13. When Jupiter is in the Sixth house, Retrograde, and the Lord of the second Peregrine, and no benevolent Fixed Star to help, the Native will be very poor and necessitous.

14. He that has Mars in his Ascendant shall be exposed to many dangers, and commonly receives, at some time, a great scar or cut on his face.

15. Mercury mixing his beams with Mars is a great argument of a violent death.

16. If Jupiter and the Moon in any nativity shall be very weak and afflicted though other positions seem never so premising, yet the Native shall be exceedingly unhappy.

17. When Venus is with Saturn and beholds the Lord of the Ascendant, the Native is inclined to Sodomy, or at least shall love old, hard-favored women, or poor dirty winches.

18. When Venus and Jupiter shall be in the Seventh, the Moon beholding them in her own dignities, and the Dragon's Head joined with them or with Mercury, the Native shall get a great Estate by means of his wives.

19. The Moon full of Light in Conjunction with Mars makes the Native to be counted a fool; but if she be void of Light and with Saturn, he is so indeed.

---

[6] These evil effects would be much modified should there be a Trine or Sextile of Jupiter to the Hyleg or Ascendant in such a figure.

20. Venus in the heart of the Sun gives vast honors and dignities. The same may be hoped for if a Planet[7] with the Fixed Star called *Cor Leonis* behold the Moon.

21. The Moon in the Seventh house renders Natives subject to the Falling-sickness, and sometimes when she is in the Ascendant, but generally she makes them fools if she be afflicted.[8]

22. Bastards and supposititious children have frequently the Ascendant in aspect with the Moon and not with the significator of the Father; and for the most part attended with indications of some great misfortunes, and either there is no agreement between the Lord of the fourth, the Lord of the second, and the Moon, or else Venus is joined with Mars or Mercury.

23. When Jupiter shall be in the tenth in Trine of Mars and strong; and the Sun with the Dragon's Head, and the Moon with *Cor Leonis*, such Native, though the son of the meanest peasant, shall be wonderfully exalted.

24. When any Planet shall be partly on the cusp of the Seventh in his own House, the Native's death will be of the nature of that Planet and Place.

25. The Infortunes in Angles denote a public death or a sudden one; the Sun there, afflicted, it shall be by some weapon or burning; the Moon, by hanging or drowning, according to circumstances.

---

[7] Cardan evidently means a Fortune, though he writes "a planet."

[8] The Moon governs the age of childhood and her effects are powerful on the weak-minded, hence the term "lunatic."

26. Sol and Mars peregrine or the Dragon's Tail in the second signifies the Native shall squander away his substance or Estate foolishly.

27. When the Moon in Opposition to the Sun is joined with nebulous stars, the Native will have some defect in his sight; if the Moon in the seventh be afflicted by both the Infortunes and if their rays are very strong, he will be blind.

28. The compound rays of Jove, Venus, Mercury, and the Moon give the greatest grace and sweetness of speech, and therefore when Jupiter shall be in Virgo and the Moon in Pisces, it is an opportune time for the birth of a Poet. Poets are always born, not made.

29. That person will scarce make a prosperous end or persevere long in any eminent degree who has not some of his Ancestors' Genitures to sympathize with and assist his own.

30. The fifth sign from the Ascendant signifies the Native's children because it is of the same nature as the Sign on the Ascendant, and if two signs shall be in the Ascendant, the children will be of humors and manners exceedingly different, the one from the other; for the same reason the ninth house signifies grand-children.

31. The Moon with the Dragon's Tail in a Nativity gives suspicion of the mother's honesty and hints that the child is none of the reputed father's begetting; however, it will prove ill-mannered and for the most part unfortunate.

32. Whoever has Jupiter in aspect with the Sun[9], will be

---

[9] More especially in Square, Opposition or other evil aspect.

proud and haughty and yet shall have little cause for it unless they happen to be in reception.

33. The Nativities of women in matters pertaining to life are like those of men, but as to fortune, wholly unlike, and touching manners, after a middle kind, neither wholly agreeable nor wholly contrary.

34. A woman that has Mars with the Moon is right; I'll warrant her.

35. In complete Nativities the Moon returns to the sign ascending at conception, or its opposite, or to the body or aspect of some Planet with whom she was at the conception, or to her own sign, and generally the Ascendant at birth is the Moon's place at conception, or its opposite, or the place of the Lord of the New Moon foregoing the conception, yet there are sober genitures too, when the Sun comes to the place of the Ascendant or its Lord, etc.

36. When Mars or the Moon shall be with the Dragon's Head or Tail in the twelfth, and Sol and Jupiter in the fourth house. the Native will be hunch-backed.

37. When Mars is Lord of a Woman's Ascendant, and Venus posited in it, or Venus is Lady of it, and Mars in it, or Mars Lord of the Ascendant in the Mid-heaven, it is more than probable she will Cuckold her husband.[10]

38. The Lord of the Ascendant in the Combust Way

---

[10] Mars conjoined with Venus in square or opposition thereto, is considered significantly evil in a female geniture unless there are excellent configurations and positions of the fortunes and luminaries to mitigate the evils foreshadowed.

shows that the Native will be much entangled and pestered with business.

39. If Infortunes be in the tenth house peregrine, and not friendly to the Ascendent, the Native will be always full of suspicions and jealousies.

40. All Planets above the Earth make a man illustrious and generally known far and near, and being all swift in motion, render him dextrous and nimble in the dispatch of affairs.[11]

41. Those that have the Moon, Lady of the Ascendant under the Earth, with the Tail of the Lion[12] and the Virgin's Head,[13] the Sun in the sixth, and Saturn or Mars in their own dignities in the Angles of the seventh will always be very infirm and weak.

42. Mercury in Pisces lays an impediment on the tongue, making a man absurd in his speech and uttering unawares what he does not conceive in his mind; so if that sign ascend.

43. Whoever is born on the day of the Vernal Equinox at noon shall by that testimony alone become great in the world.

44. Women that have their Ascendant, Moon, Mars, Ve-

---

[11] Many planets in fixed signs are also said to produce fame.

[12] Deneb (*Cauda Leonis*), a Fixed Star of the second magnitude in 19°53' of Virgo, of the nature of Saturn and Venus. Its effect is unfortunate and said to make one publicly disgraceful.

[13] Vindemiatrix, a Fixed atar of the 3d magnitude in 8°24' of Virgo, of the nature of Saturn, Venus and Mercury. It is mischievous and unfortunate in effect.

nus, and Mercury in double-bodied signs have generally very evil qualities.

45. Jupiter very potent in a geniture always promises some extraordinary happiness, and if he be in the Mid-heaven near the cusp in Capricorn he gives a great deal of good fortune by means of violence and power under pretense of justice, but the same will have an unfortunate issue.

46. Famous are those persons in whose Nativities the Moon receives the light of many Planets or is joined to some powerful Royal Fixed Star.[14]

47. When Sol and Jupiter rule in the ninth, and over the places of Mercury, the Moon, and Ascendant, and do behold each other, such a Native's words will be regarded as oracles.

48. Jupiter and the Sun in the second house give a gallant, noble, free spirit; but Saturn and Mars, or Saturn with Mercury in the seventh, render men sordidly covetous.

49. When the Lord of the figure of a Nativity shall be Retrograde, and both ways Cadent, the Native will be a weak, poor-spirited, dejected fellow, bringing nothing to perfection.

50. An Artist may more easily and certainly judge of a man's nativity than of the weather, because he knows the time of birth, but not that of the gathering together of vapors.

51. Sol in Leo alone raises a man, at least scarce ever suffers him to want or beg, and if the same sign ascend, it

---

[14] Such as Mirach, Rigel, or Sirius.

buoys up his spirit with hopes, and makes him master of more than ordinary reason.[15]

52. If Cancer ascend, and the Moon be in Moveable or Common signs, especially remote from an Angle, the Native is credulous, light, and inconstant.

53. Venus in the house or exaltation of Mars is always a filthy lust.

54. The Moon in Aquarius or Pisces makes the Native to be disliked by Princes, Grandees and the upper ten.

55. When the Lord of the Mid-heaven separates by Retrogradation from the Lord of the Ascendant, the Prince, King, or Ruler, shall be averse to the Native, but if on the other side the Lord of the Ascendant being Retrograde forsakes the Lord of the tenth, then the Native shall hate his Prince, King, or Governors; the like is to be understood of other houses according to their respective significations.

56. A Native of a City having the same sign and degree ascending with that City, shall in that place, by that alone grow great and eminent.

57. When the Lord of the second applies to the Lord of the Ascendant, especially if the Lord of the Ascendant be Jupiter, the Native shall, all his life time, be happy in acquiring riches even to admiration.

58. When the Lord of the Ascendant beholds the Sun with a friendly aspect or is Oriental next to the Sun, or joined

---

[15] A man born under this configuration is generally difficult to overcome either with words or by force.

with the Lord of the tenth, the Native will be much beloved by Kings and great people; for the cause of which favor consider the nature of the said Lord of the Ascendant and his place.

59. When several children have the same accidents and fortune, if it be in their childhood, it may be shown by the genitures of their parents; or if in their old age, we may conclude the Nativities of their Parents were so powerful that they assimilate their Nativities between themselves and suit them to the disposition of Children in the Paternal Figure.[16]

60. Mars in moveable Signs makes people hasty and choleric, but nowhere more than in Cancer, nor less than in Virgo, but in the former he generally makes the tongue more foolish and impertinent.

61. Saturn in the twelfth threatens the gout; in the sixth some lasting disease or tedious imprisonments.

62. If the Moon be between Mars and Sol or with them, the Native will almost exchange his cradle for a grave, being very short-lived.

63. If the Moon separates from an Infortune, the Native will suffer many diseases in nursing, and afflictions afterwards.

64. Whoever has Venus not well posited, within the rays of Mars, unfortunate, will assuredly suffer a world of mischief and troubles by means of love.[17]

---

[16] It is marvelous to note the sympathies which nearly always exist between the nativities of parents and children.

[17] More especially will the native suffer if the geniture be that of a female.

65. Watery Signs, but especially and above all others, Scorpio, make traitors; and therefore if the Moon Lady of the Ascendant be in that viperous sign; the native will betray, or prove a traitor to his master; and if the same position happen in the radix of a City, its inhabitants will be rebellious against their Princes or Governors.

66. Mars is seldom joined with Mercury for good, for he makes people naughty and impudent, yet industrious in Art, whence it comes to pass that the best Artists are too often the worst men.

67. Mars unfortunate in the ninth signifies liars and atheists.

68. He that has Mercury well posited but the Moon afflicted shall understand well, but deliberate ill, and therefore such, though they may advise others excellently, yet shall manage their own affairs foolishly.

69. When Venus shall be too powerful[18] in a geniture, and in places (terms) of the Infortunes, inconveniences are to be feared from unlawful loves.

70. When the Moon and Mercury, and the Lord of the Ascendant shall be all in double-bodied Signs, the Native will be naturally addicted to old opinions and curious religious notions.

71. When Saturn and Mars behold each other, and the Luminaries be posited in the sixth, eighth, or twelfth houses, the Native shall labor under some incurable disease and lead a life wholly miserable.

---

[18] Angular.

72. When the Moon is in the Mid-heaven in Capricorn, and Saturn or Mars in the fourth, the Native will be infamous, and so much the worse if Mars be in Taurus, and the Moon in Scorpio, for then many troubles will attend him during his whole life.

73. When Venus is with Saturn and Mars, and in opposition to the place of the Moon, the Native shall be but a fool, yet think himself a Philosopher.

74. For the profession or Art of the Native we must consider the Planet which being Oriental first makes its egress from under the Sun beams, and if with this there be another in the Mid-heaven that beholds the Moon, take him for an Assistant, but if there be no such Planet coming from under the Sun beams take him that is in the Mid-heaven, and if there be none therein posited then the Lord of it, and the places of Mars, Venus, and Mercury, but when these happen to be many, the Native will practice several Arts; now the Art a Native practices is much affected by the series of revolutions, which if they agree with his Nativity, he will be delighted with it; otherwise he will do it against his will.

75. A prime cause of men leading single lives is the combustion of the Moon in their Nativities with Saturn[19], or eminently afflicted by him, so in women it a Planet be cornbust or the Sun in Taurus greatly afflicted.

76. Mars and Mercury evilly disposed and in conjunction with the Moon signifies Thieves and Robbers, but if Saturn behold them, or be in the seventh, they will suffer according to their deserts, and therefore whenever you see indica-

---

[19] This causes men to be of solitary habits.

tions of grievous crimes, consider whether the Infortunes are strong or not, and oppress the Sun, Moon, or Lord of the Ascendant; or if the Lord of the Ascendant be combust, or an enemy to the Moon, for then undoubtedly the Native will suffer for his villainy.

77. When the Moon is joined to Saturn in an Angle, the Native though a Grandee will be reduced to poverty.

78. Let him that has Mars in the second house beware of concerning himself in merchandise.

79. He that hath a Nativity unfortunate for riches and honor, and yet the Moon in conjunction with an eminent propitious Fixed Star, shall unexpectedly become potent, and again fall to misery, but to judge of the greatness of the event consider the state of the Moon.

80. When Venus is in the eleventh, Mercury in the twelfth, the Sun in the horoscope, Jupiter in the second, Saturn in the sixth, and the Moon in the ninth, so many and great accidents will happen to the Native that his life may justly be esteemed prodigious.

81. Saturn, Mars, and the Dragon's Head in the fourth betoken sudden Death.

82. When the Moon in a nocturnal Geniture passes by her beams from Mars to Saturn, many inconveniences will happen to the Native, chiefly occasioned by women.

83. Those persons are like to prove very learned in whose nativities, Saturn, Venus, Jupiter, and the Moon, do exactly behold Mercury, provided that neither Saturn nor the

Moon be posited in the Ascendant, and that there be no Planet in an Angle, for any Planet strong in an Angle is an impediment to wisdom.

84. When the Sun peregrine in *Corde Coeli* shall be in square of the Moon in the seventh, the Native will come to be the chief of his family or faction, but shall die suddenly.[20]

85. In all Nativities examine exactly all the Moon's condition in relation to the three ways whereby she is exalted, for 'tis very necessary.[21]

86. When Infortunes are in Angles, and Fortunes in Succedent houses, or the Moon combust, and the Lord of her place strong and happy, or Jupiter Cadent, and his disposition well-dignified, the Native from a sad mean condition and great misery shall rise to a considerable grandeur and felicity, and so on the contrary.

87. When the Moon, Venus and Mars are altogether in conjunction, 'tis time to bring Neros and such cursed monsters of mankind into the world; the Native's manners are prodigiously wicked.

88. Jupiter elevated and a little infortunate destroys the Native's children, but preserves his estate; if he be descending and low and not unfortunate, he gives children but not an estate.

---

[20] The Luminaries in Square presignify violent or sudden death unless the benefic rays of Jupiter interpose.

[21] The Moon is exalted or dignified as follows: 1. By house in Cancer. 2. By exaltation in Taurus. 3. By triplicity when she is in Taurus, Virgo or Capricorn. The Moon is also held to be propitious when she is swift in motion and increasing in light, provided other testimonies agree.

89. When Saturn does not threaten a violent death, yet if he be in or lord of the seventh or eighth houses[22], he signifies the Native shall die for grief of mind.[23]

90. Infortunes peregrine in the seventh house, having dominion in the Ascendant, denote the deaths of the Native's wives or enemies.[24]

91. It is next to impossible that they have never a planet above the Earth, nor in the Ascendant of their nativities, should either live long or accomplish any great matters in the world.

92. The number of a Native's wives (where only one at once is lawful) is to be found out not only from the concourse of the Planets or Common signs, but with what you must consider that fit applications of the Moon to Planets at ripe years[25], and testimonies of the Death of wives do also concur.

93. When Mars and Mercury afflict the Lord of the seventh, being elevated above him, the Native will kill his wife or his enemy[26], even though it be with poison, especially if either of them have power in the Ascendant.

94. If in a woman's nativity Mars shall be under the Sun

---

[22] Provided he be Anareta.

[23] Or of such diseases as Saturn signifies. Violent chills, etc., having always due regard to his position and configuration in the figure under consideration.

[24] Or partners.

[25] After the native shall have arrived at the age of puberty.

[26] Or partner.

beams, she will be apt to play the Harlot with her Servants and mean fellows[27]; but if Venus be true, then she will trade discreetly with Nobles and gallants of quality.

95. Infortunes afflicting the place of children, if they be but a little weak, the Native may have children; if much debilitated, the children he has will die; if they be very weak, he will be wholly barren.

96. When the Lord of the Geniture is an Infortune and does not behold the place of children, or being a Fortune beholds them with an Aspect of hatred, the Native will never love his children as he ought to do.

97. When Mercury is under the Earth he has greater efficacy in relation to giving Arts and Sciences, but in respect of eloquence he is best when he is above the Earth.

98. When Mars is exactly on the cusp of the Mid-heaven, and has no dominion in the Ascendant, if the Native live to any considerable age, 'tis much to be feared that he will be killed.

99. When it happens that the Significators of persons of quality well posited in their own genitures are such as were unfortunate in the Nativities of their Parents, it signifies that they shall spin out a laborious life as to riches and honor to a considerable age, and then by successive increases shall attain to great Estates and Eminence, when 'tis evident that the lives of no persons may be more unlike to each other than theirs who were born at the same time.

---

[27] Provided always there be no strong benefic aspect of Jupiter with the Sun.

100. Nativities which can never be good are such as have both the Infortunes in the same place joined to one of the Luminaries, or when the Infortunes single are singly joined to the Luminaries, or when the Moon is under the Sun beams with Saturn or Mars, or where all the Planets are in the third, sixth, eighth, or twelfth houses, or when the Infortunes are in Angles, and the Luminaries and Fortunes Cadent, or when the Luminaries only are Cadent and all the other Planets Retrograde, or when both the Luminaries and both the Fortunes are afflicted, or when only Mars is above the Earth the other Planets not being mutually joined nor in Angles.

Aphorisms
Concerning Revolutions

1. Revolutions may be said to be accomplished five ways: first, by the return of the Sun to the sane point, which is most valid; secondly, the return of the center of a Planet to the same place of the Ecliptic, of which kind that of the Moon first, and then those of Saturn and Jupiter are chief; thirdly, the return of the center of some smaller Circle to the game place; fourthly, the return of a Planet to his place in a smaller circle; fifthly, the return of a Planet wherewith he was in the beginning joined as it is the place of another Planet.

2. When the Dragon's Tail in a Nativity unfortunately beholds the Lord of the Ascendant and in a Revolution the Moon shall be joined therewith, and the Lord of the House of Death being then in the place of an Infortune in the Radix, shall likewise behold it, the Party that year will die.[1]

3. When the Infortunes are strong in the Radix, and the Moon applies to a powerful Fixed Star of the Nature of Mars in a Revolution, the Party will be apt to commit manslaughter that year, or be in danger about it.[2]

4. Revolutions may produce effects happening in the

---

[1] Provided always primary directions coincide with the other testimonies.

[2] A violent nature, frequently shown by the Infortunes when strong in a Nativity, if devoid of the controlling benefic rays of Jupiter, would be stirred up, and influenced to action by such an application of the Moon in a Revolutionary figure.

years following, either because one year is preparative to another, or because the Nativity decrees what the Revolution perfects, or by reason of the greatness of the event as death, or of the causes, as when the Sun is exactly in opposition of Jupiter.

5. When the Ascendant of a Revolution is the same with that of the person's Nativity, something promised in the geniture happens, but much more certainly if the Moon shall be also in her place of the geniture, or the Lord of the Ascendant in a place partially behold the same house of the Radix.

6. If in a Revolution the Lord of the Geniture Retrograde (if he be one of the Inferiors), begins to be under the Sun beams, or (if he be one of the Superiors) begins to be under afflicted by an Infortune, you may expect some danger of your life that year.

7. When Jupiter in a Revolution beholds the Moon or Venus, or be in an Angle in either of their places in the Radix, it inclines the Party, if of fit age that year, to marry.[3]

8. When in a person's Revolution whose only significator of life was debilitated in the Radix, the Fortunes shall be combust in any house but the Ascendant, and the Infortunes being above the Earth shall behold the Sun, Ascendant and Moon, or the Moon be under the Earth, such person without any ill direction may die that year.[4]

---

[3] And if marriage is denied by the nativity he will be inclined to live with a mistress.

[4] This statement should be received with great caution. The Astrologer should never judge of death save by primary directions which correspond with secondary directions in showing evidence of final dissolution. It is of course well to consider the Revolutionary figure in connection with the directions.

9. If a Geniture be weak as to life, and three Planets be joined in a Revolution, there is imminent danger of some eminent disease, especially if they happen in the sixth house.

10. When at ripe Age a Revolution shall have Venus in Sextile of Mercury, who was joined to her in the Genesis in the same place, the Native will be strangely haunted with wanton thoughts and venereal imaginations, and if they shall be in Conjunction in the same place where before they were Sextile, he shall that year enjoy some mistress that he is much enamored of.

11. When in the hour of a Revolution the Superior Planets or others shall be joined in the place of a Radical Significator, expect from thence some notable matter to happen of that kind which is thereby naturally promised.

12. When the Moon is joined with Saturn in a Revolution, and he casts a Square to the Ascendant, such person shall that year suffer in his body by reason of a disease of his mind.[5]

13. The additions that are made by the procession of the Sun in an annual Revolution, transfer the significations for near upon so many days after the Revolution, as there are years past.

14. When the Moon agreeing with Saturn in the Radix, or being with any other Planet in his dignities, if she happen in a Revolution (after the age of forty years) to be corporally joined with Saturn in the same latitude, or being full of light shall be in opposition to him and in contrary latitude from the

---

[5] Or vertigo.

sixth house to the eighth, the Native will undoubtedly fall into some strange disease and die thereof.[6]

15. When the houses of the Ascendant or Moon in the Radix shall be in Square or Opposition to the Infortunes in a Revolution, the Native will suffer much trouble, but if the Moon be in Conjunction with them, then he shall do much mischief to other people, but if besides this the Infortunes are Lords of inimical places, he shall both do damage to others and suffer much himself.

16. The particular times of accidents happening are to be found out from annual and monthly Revolutions and transits.[7]

17. Fatal will that year be to the Native's health, when in the Revolution many of the Hylegicals come to bad places of the Figure, or to the Aspects of the Infortunes.

18. If any Planet be afflicted in an annual revolution, the effects will appear when he shall apply by body, Square or Opposition to the Planet that is Lord of the sign wherein he is.

19. Diseases are for the most part of the nature of the Lord of the sixth house, or the Planet therein posited as well in Revolutions as Nativities.

20. The Revolution of a year is one thing in time, which is the return of the Sun to the same point from the Equinoc-

---

[6] Provided always primary directions influence such.

[7] The Moon by her transits influences the lesser events of life; the greater Luminary and the planets by their transits, influence the greater events of life.

tial, another thing in the world, which is its return to the same Fixed Star, and yet another thing in Nativities, which is its return to its former place, but with the addition of so much of the Ecliptic as he passes through in one natural day.

Aphorisms Relating to Decumbitures, Diseases, Physic, Etc.

1. In sickness, the Ascendant[1] shall signify the Patient, the seventh house the disease, the Luminaries the Patient's strength, the Infortunes the strength of the disease, but the eighth house has always a share in the signification.[2]

2. When the Moon applies to Planets of a nature contrary to that of the distemper, especially if they be Fortunes, the disease will be changed for the better.

3. When the Moon in the beginning of a sickness (which is called the Decumbiture of the Patient) shall be either under the Sun beams or with the Dragon's Tail, Saturn or Mars, it threatens extraordinary danger, and if the party be old, even her Conjunction with Jupiter, Mercury, or Venus is not without peril; the same but nothing so grievous may be feared when she is in Square or Opposition to any of them, but if besides all this she shall happen to have been in their places in the Patient's geniture, he will certainly die.

4. Mars, Jupiter, and Venus rule the blood; Mars and Sol, choler; the Moon and Venus, phlegm; Saturn and Mercury, melancholy; and Mars and Mercury with the Sun, black choler.

---

[1] And its Lord.

[2] The seventh house and its Lord signify the physician.

5. Saturn causes long diseases; Venus indifferent; Mercury various ones; the Moon such as return after a certain time, as Vertigoes, Falling-sickness, etc.[3] Jupiter and Sol give short diseases, but Mars the most acute of all.

6. When you find the Figure at the beginning of a grievous distemper to appear much more mild and favorable than the distemper, you may conclude the disease contracts its malignity from the Nativity, the principal places fall upon some disastrous configurations.

7. It is necessary to consider the Lunations preceding the disease and thence likewise to take indications of the Patient's condition.

8. If you find a person after the age of 50 years labor under strong and frequent diseases, you may conclude the significator of life in his Radix to be sorely afflicted by the body or aspects of one of the Infortunes.

9. When the Moon is in a fixed sign, physic works the less, and if in Aries, Taurus, or Capricorn, it will be apt to prove nauseous and very distasteful to the Patient.

10. In Purging, 'tis best that both the Moon and Lord of the Ascendant descend and be under the Earth, in vomiting that they ascend.

11. In Purging, Vomiting, Bleeding, making use of issues, etc., ought to be done while the Moon is in moist signs, the chief of which is Pisces, the next Cancer.

12. The significator of life in the Radix being strong in

---

[3] And all diseases proceeding from excess of moisture, humor, etc.

natural diseases helps very much, but in casualties, little or nothing.

13. When the Moon is with Venus, Choler is better and more safely expelled; and when she is with Jupiter, Melancholy.

14. Every immoderate Position of the Heavens to persons weak and abed brings death; to others, violent accidents and grievous calamities.

15. If a disease begin when the Moon is in Opposition to the Sun, 'tis by reason of superfluity of humors; if she suffer an eclipse, the same time 'tis for weakness of the Spirits and Vital power.

16. The Infortunes being Oriental, causes Diseases; Occidental, defect.

17. Venus with Saturn in the seventh and Mars elevated above them both, causes barrenness in men, and Abortions in women.

18. Sagittary and Gemini signify Diseases that come with falling, as Swooning, Falling-sickness, Suffocations of the womb, etc.

19. When at the beginning of a disease the Luminaries are both with the Infortunes, or in Opposition to them, the sick will very hardly escape.

20. From the Moon's applications to the Fortunes or good aspect of the Sun, the same being neither contrary to the disease, nor afflicted, nor in the power of the Infortunes, health may be expected, but by her going to the Infortunes of

like nature with the disease, or ill beams of the Sun, death is to be feared.

21. Cold and dry diseases, such as are naturally long, are increased by Saturn; but those that are short, hot and dry, from Mars.

22. A Conjunction of the Luminaries in Aries causes alteration and death; if Venus and Mercury be there Retrograde; the like if it happen in Scorpio or Virgo or in any humane sign; so likewise if such Conjunction fall in the sixth, seventh, or eighth house of the figure of the Decumbiture within the Aspect of an Infortune, the Patient will be in great danger.

23. Mars in the Ascendant in a Decumbiture, makes the disease, swift, violent[4], afflicting the upper parts and disturbing the mind; and if besides this, the dispositors of the Luminaries and Ascendant happen to be afflicted, death will follow; the like if both the Luminaries be Cadent from Angles, and not assisted by the Fortunes; but if in such a position, the Fortunes strong shall have dominion in two places, the disease will be changed from Acute to Chronic, and the Patient will escape beyond hope.

24. From the first hour of the day (or one in the morning inclusive) till six, blood predominates, whence morning sleeps become so sweet and pleasant; from thence to noon, Choler; afternoon, Phlegm; and from the beginning of the night till mid-night, Melancholy.

25. Saturn in Fiery Signs when the Sun is weak causes

---

[4] Symptoms of fever will probably set in.

hectic fevers; Jupiter, sanguinary ones; and if Mars behold him, Putrid ones: Mars in such signs gives burning fevers of all sorts; Venus, ephemeral fevers; and if the rays of Mars be mixed, putrid ones from phlegm; Mercury, mixed ones; but if the Moon be joined with him she makes pituitous fevers from the corruption of the humors; Saturn mixing signification with Mars causes Melancholy fevers, and if Mars be under the Sun in the sixth or twelfth house in Fiery Signs, or being so posited shall cast his beams on the Significator of life, or the Lord of the Ascendant of the Revolution, or if the Lord of the Ascendant or Significator of life apply to his aspects by direction, it occasions burning pernicious fevers and like to venomous ones; but if to these, Saturn or the Dragon's Head or Tail, or Venus Combust be added, or if these Planets shall be posited in Scorpio or Leo, the fever will be altogether pestilential.

26. Mischievous fevers are caused when the Sun is afflicted in Leo, but if otherwise he be fortified they seldom happen, because the matter then corrupts and is carried off, unless by chance.

27. Watery signs threaten Putrid fevers of very bad continuance if Mars (especially combust) have any rule in them, but earthly signs are altogether free from putrid fevers.

28. It will be a fatal time to suffer amputation or lose a member when the Moon is in an oblique sign under the Sun beams and opposed to Mars.[5]

29. A tedious travail and delivery in childbirth is to be

---

[5] Ptolemy writes in *Tetrabiblos*: "Pierce not with iron that part of the body which may be governed by the sign actually occupied by the Moon."

expected when the Moon is aspected by the Infortunes, and in an oblique sign, and a Planet Retrograde or slow of motion in the Ascendant.

30. Venus is cold in the second degree, and moist in the third; the Moon cold in the third, and moist in the fourth; Jupiter hot in the second, and moist in the first; the Sun hot in the third, and dry in the second; Mars dry in the third, and hot in the fourth; and Saturn both cold and dry in the fourth.

31. The special Significator of a disease is that unfortunate Planet from whom the Significator separates by a bad aspect; and the Lord of the Ascendant shows the cause of the grief if he be found anywhere unfortunate.

32. If the Lord of the Ascendant be an Infortune the sick will be unruly, but if he be a Fortune he will readily take what is prescribed.

33. The fifth house and its Lord show the medicines and nature, whether good or evil, proper or improper.

34. As the Revolution of a year as to its ill significations happens according to the directions from the geniture, so the decumbiture as to its worse significations is regulated by the Revolution according to Lunar directions.

35. Several Planets being significators show that the distemper is complicated of several diseases.

36. The Signification of the disease in double-bodied signs signifies a relapse, or that it will change into some other distemper.

37. The disease is desperate, when the significator of the

sick either in his Nativity or decumbiture, has dominion in the fourth house.

38. That sign in which the significator of the disease is posited, and that to which he casts any aspect, show the members or parts of the body principally afflicted.

39. When Mercury is unfortunate he prejudices the fantasy and inward faculties, and thence threatens madness, etc., but so much the worse if Mars be the Planet that afflicts him, for then if he be in an Earthy Sign it threatens patient will make away with himself.

40. It is a very bad sign when the Significator of the sickness is in the sixth, or the Lord of the sixth in the eighth, or the Lord of the eighth in the sixth house.

41. Mercury significator of a disease in aspect with Saturn, or Saturn significator in aspect of Mercury, gives suspicion of witchcraft and enchantment.[6]

---

[6] The theory of witchcraft is held up to ridicule by most orthodox scientific men of the present day who have not carefully investigated the matter, but it may perhaps be advantageous to some students of natural philosophy to bear in mind that Saturn, amongst other things, is the significator of the occult, that he gives great reflective and concentrative powers; and Mercury signifies, amongst other things, the magnetic fluid or odylic force, also that subtlety and rapidity of thought necessary to be exerted at the right time in all magnetic experiments where the sensitive is to be acted upon at a distance from the operator, as would usually be the case in witchcraft or enchantment. These two planets, therefore, which Cardan quotes are the very significators of the subtle power and means which must be exerted in order to bring about the magnetic effect termed by our forefathers, witchcraft, and which modern occultists recognize as the outcome of black magic, or evil magnetism. If witchcraft, or rather an occult influence of an evil nature, be shown in a decumbiture, the opera-

42. A chronical disease (that is, a disease which usually continues above a month) is ruled by the motion of the Sun; acute diseases (which are more sharp and violent but less lasting) by the motion of the Moon, according to whose swifter or slower motion the critical times are either hastened or retarded[7], the same being when the Moon comes to a sign contrary in both qualities to that in which she was in the beginning of the disease.

43. For curing a member, the Moon and Lord of the Ascendant should be tree from impediment, the sign that governs the part ascending and the Moon posited in it, and when you think to do any good to your eyes, let the Moon be fortunate, increasing in light and by no means in a sign of the Earthy Triplicity.

44. Even the Fortunes in diseases may became Infortunes, viz., when the disease itself is of their nature, or of the nature of things by them signified, and in such case the Infortunes may be said to be fortunes, for contraries are cured by contraries.

---

tor can often be discovered by a consideration of the fourth and twelfth houses, together with positions and configurations of their lords, in the figure, having due regard to Saturn and Mercury, and comparing carefully with the Radix and Revolutionary Figure for the year. It is advisable to consider also the position and configurations of Herschel.

[7] Much excellent matter is given in Claudius Dariot, *Judicial Astrology*, on the influence and powers of the Moon with regard to critical periods of sickness (London, 1598).

Aphorisms Concerning Elections

1. An Election signifies nothing or very little unless it correspond with the Nativity, and time wherein you elect.[1]

2. It you would have anything kept secret let the Moon be under the Sun beams when you do it.[2]

3. Make no new clothes, nor first put them on when the Moon is in Scorpio, especially if she be full of light and beheld of Mars, for they will be apt to be torn and quickly worn out.

4. When in an Election you cannot fit the Moon to two Planets that you have occasion for, at once, join her to some Fixed Star that is of the nature of them both.

5. When you would suddenly finish a thing, place the Moon and Significator in Moveable Signs, but if you would have your work last long, let then be in Fixed ones, and for this reason it becomes so difficult for a man to attain to do both.

---

[1] "In all authors that ever I yet met with I find there can be no time elected (in this, our astrological way of electing) advantageous to anyone whose nativity or time of birth is not exactly known, for according unto it must you frame your election, together with respect to the revolutions of the year; and Zael, Bonatus, Messahalla and Dariot say that in case the nativity of a man cannot be obtained, respect must be had to the time of the question."—Wm. Ramsey, *Astrologia Restorata* (London, 1654).

[2] Ramsey, in his Table of Elections in *Astrologia Restorata*, under Moon conjoined to Sun, writes: "Begin nothing but that thou wouldest have hidden and secret."

6. The best election a man can make is the place of his habitation; for if the Ascendant of the City he dwells in be the place of his Ascendant, he will have his health well; if the Mid-heaven, he will come to preferment; if it be the place of the Sun in the Nativity, he will undoubtedly obtain honor and dignities; if of Jupiter, he will grow rich; if of the Moon, he will be very happy in most respects there.

7. Every man's geniture in some things agrees with, and in some differs from another's, we should therefore deal with people (as to important natters) only in things wherein their Nativities sympathize with ours, but in other things to forbear, and indeed we ought generally to avoid the society of a person the Lord of whose Ascendant is an Infortune and joined with the Dragon's Tail or any malevolent Fixed Star, for unless there be a great agreement between our Nativities they will do us sane mischief, though perhaps against their will.

8. When the significators of journeys are in watery signs and the Infortunes (or the Fortunes themselves unfriendly posited) be elevated above them, the querent will be much troubled in his journeys with bad weather and tempests, and note that the causes or business of journeys is to be discovered from the dispositors of the significators.

9. You may sometimes use the Infortunes as Physicians do poisons, for they produce strong effects; but use them like those, sparingly and with caution.

10. News or reports raised and spread abroad while the Moon is in the beginning of Scorpio or Capricorn are generally false, but if she be with Jupiter in a masculine sign they are like to prove true.

11. Begin not to build while the Moon is in Scorpio or Pisces or when a southern sign ascends, nor let the Moon or lord of the fourth apply to a Retrograde Planet, for it threatens that such edifices shall soon fall or be ruined.[3]

12. At Play and in War it is said that it is considerable for a man to have his face look towards a friendly Part of Heaven, and that if both parties do so, the contest will be tedious; if neither of them, then both in battle will be much prejudiced, and in gaming there will be little won on either side, but if one of them only look that way, he will soon conquer his antagonist.

13. In every Election, let the Moon and Lord of the Ascendant be free from impediment or affliction.

14. But if when the Moon suffers some impediment from another Planet, thou art forced on that day to make an election, let a sign ascend that is either the house or exaltation of that Planet so impediting.

15. It is best to undertake journeys when the significators are in moveable signs, for they signify celerity and return with dispatch of business, but fixed signs in such cases are very bad, so also it is if the Lord of the Ascendant or Moon happen to be in the sixth, eighth, or twelfth houses.

16. It is an undeniable thing (in general) to deliver a peti-

---

[3] Or the habitation will not, owing to circumstances, be enjoyed long by the person who elects such an unpropitious time for his work. "To every thing there is a season, and a time for every purpose under the heaven. . . .A time to cast away stones and a time to gather stones together" (Ecclesiastes, c. a, vs. 1 and 5). "Fools build houses for wise men to live in" (Old Proverb).

tion or request to a great person when the Moon applies to Jupiter, and he is joined with the Dragon's Head in the Mid-heaven.

Aphorisms Relating to Eclipses and Comets

1. In an Eclipse it is necessary to consider the strength of the Planet then ruling, for his significations will chiefly appear.

2. Eclipses of the Sun have powerful effects, and therefore if they fall upon a very flourishing and promising crop they generally damnify it, so that it scarce comes to anything near what might have been expected.

3. When at the time of an Eclipse the significator of life in any person's Radix shall be within the beams of the Anareta or killing Planet, or of an Infortune not friendly disposed, such native will incur extraordinary hazard of his life.

4. In general some Eclipses of the luminaries at the time or even before they happen raise showers and rain, others great droughts, some violent winds, others earthquakes, some scarcity of the fruits of the earth, others terrible fires.

5. A Comet usually foreshows the birth of some famous persons to see in some time after to happen, for he is not said to be born under it (in this sense) who is born during the time of its appearance, but he that is born in that region or country subject to such an Angle or Figure, and hath his Sun and Moon in its place, or the Luminaries and the Lord of his Ascendant, in Cardinal signs, when the Comet rises, sets or culminates, and the like.

6. A Comet in the East signifies the rise of some eminent

lawgiver; in the Mid-heaven, of some powerful King; but seldom any illustrious matter when 'tis in the West or Succedent houses.

7. Comets, when they are immoveable, signify seditions, but when moveable they denote Foreign Wars, and one Nation invading another; in Cardinal signs, the death of Princes and great men; in the ninth house, scandal or detriment to Religion; in the tenth or twelfth houses, the pestilence or scarcity of corn; and in the eleventh house, great slaughter and destruction of Noblemen.

8. If a Comet appear while a woman goes with child, if it be either in the fourth, sixth, or eighth month, such child will prove prone to anger and quarrels, and if he be of quality, to sedition.

9. No Eclipse whatsoever can threaten a scarcity or plague to the whole Earth, nor can the pestilence continue above four years in one place.

10. Eclipses in the fourth house are more strong and efficacious than in the eighth or twelfth houses, and in the Ascendant more than in the ninth or eleventh.

11. An Eclipse of the Moon extends its effects as many months, and of the Sun so many years, as it continues hours.

12. An Eclipse has a threefold effect, first powerful by reason of the conjunction or opposition in which it happens; second general, because it slowly cools, in which respect it is extended for a long time. Thirdly, power which it has from the Lord of the place where it happens and other positions at that time.

13. Eclipses operate mere forcibly in Cities, Provinces, and Kingdoms[4] than on particular persons of private condition, or even upon Kings and Princes, for their effects rather respect the multitude.

14. When Eclipses happen or Comets appear in Earthly Signs they portend barrenness and scarcity by reason of excessive droughts; when in Watery Signs by reason of too much rain; in Airy Signs they signify mighty winds, seditions and the pestilence; in Fiery Signs, terrible Wars and slaughters.

---

[4] "Earthquakes generally follow close on the heels of eclipses."—Commander Morrison, R.N., *Rules for Predicting Earthquakes*.

Aphorisms Touching Weather, Meteors, Etc.

1. When Saturn passes out of one sign into another, you may expect for several days together strange Meteors and splendid sights or apparitions in the heavens.

2. When signs very different from the common course of nature appear about the Sun, or in or about the Moon, Stars, or any part of heaven, if you observe the place where they appear, and the figure of the heaven from the beginning to the end, thou mayest come to understand what they portend.[1]

3. The Lord of the Interlunary Figure signifies very much as to the quality of the Air, and also the Planet that beholds him, especially if they be in Cardinal Signs.

---

[1] Sybilina Tiburtina, who lived in the reign of the Emperor Augustus, observed a brilliant star in the autumn of the year 4 B.C. She pointed it out to the Emperor, and told him it indicated that a child would be born of a virgin, who should be greater than he, and she urged him to worship the child (see Pearce, *Text-book of Astrology*).

It was by observing a figure of the heavens on the appearance of a strange star that the Magi knew of the birth of our Lord, for we read: "They came from the east to Jerusalem, saying, 'Where is he that is born King of the Jews, for we have seen his star in the EAST, and are come to worship him.'"—St. Matthew, c. w, verses 1 and 2. Doctor Swadling, in *Divinity an Enemy to Astrology* (London, 1653), writes as follows: "Saint Chrystom says, 'By a STAR did God direct the Gentiles, not by an ANGEL, not by a PROPHET, not by a VOICE from heaven, because he would condescend to their weakness and teach them by such things as they were most acquainted with,' and here because these Arabians were Astrologers, and well versed in the stars, he calleth them to himself by a STAR."

4. When Saturn is Combust in the houses of Mars, and Mars beholds him, he often begets conical figures which are seen in the air composed of vapors that ascend, and are signs of an earthquake to ensue.

5. Saturn and Mars, and Mars and the Sun, and Mars and Mercury, cause hail; Saturn most in summer, Sol and Mercury most in autumn, and those that cause hail in these two quarters cause snow in the winter and spring.

6. Saturn with the Luminaries, Jupiter with Mercury and Mars with Venus, make an *Apertio portarum* or an opening of the gates, and usually cause some notable change of weather.

7. When about the beginning of winter Saturn shall dispose of the Moon, expect unusual Colds with a cloudy season and rain.

8. Whenever Saturn is joined to the Sun the heat is remitted and the cold increased, which alone may be a sufficient testimony of the truth of Astrology.

9. When Mars and Mercury are joined and behold the Moon or Lord of the Ascendant in the sixth or seventh house, they portend a great drought to ensue.

10. The Star has a great efficacy upon the air, to which the Moon shall be first joined after her conjunction, opposition or square with the Sun.

11. The mixture of the beams of Jove and Mars in moist signs gives Thunder with sudden showers.

12. Jupiter naturally raises North Winds; Saturn, East-

erly; Mars, Western; Venus, Southern; and Mercury, Mixed winds, according as he applies to other Planets.[2]

---

[2] Dr. Goad, author of *Astro-Meteorologica* (London, 1686), bears out the aphorisms touching the weather.

Some Aphorisms Relating to Husbandry

1. If you prune your vines when the Moon is at full in Taurus, Leo, Scorpio, Sagittarius, neither worms nor birds will infest your grapes.

2. Graft not Trees, the Moon waning, or not to be seen, and if you shear sheep in her increase their wool will grow again the better.

3. Fruits and Wood for use should be cut in the decrease of the Moon, but if you would have Timber to keep long, fell it towards the latter end of the winter, the Moon being under the Earth, and beheld by Saturn, for that will prevent its rotting, and render it exceedingly hard and durable.

4. But fire wood and what you would have grow quickly again, cut when the Moon is above the Earth in the first quarter either joined to Venus or Jupiter.

5. Sow or Plant when the Moon is in Taurus, Virgo or Scorpio in good Aspect of Saturn, but when she is in Cancer, set or sow all kinds of pulse, and in Libra or Capricorn, dress your gardens and trim your small trees and shrubs.

6. Saturn in fixed signs causes scarcity of corn, dear years, and the death of many men.

7. When Trees blossom they are most apt to be affected with injuries from the Heavens, for then they are like teeming women and when they have put out their fruits like Nurses

giving suck, which can endure more than when they went with child; and therefore if Eclipses happen while a tree is so blooming, it most times causes a scarcity of that kind of fruit that year, and indeed the plenty of corn and fruit is not much discovered from the Vernal figure of Revolution of the World, as from the temperature of the air, in moisture, dryness, or inequality, as also from the new and full Moons, and risings of the Stars; and Eclipses, especially happening then while things respectively blossom.

8. A Malevolent Planet being Lord of the year, though fortunate, generally hurts all fruits of the Earth, but those particularly signified by himself.

Aphorisms Relating to
General Accidents

1. Saturn obtains Kingdom or Supremacy of power by labor, fraud, and infamy; Mars by valor, rapine and cruelty; but Jupiter by Justice and great opinion of goodness and honesty.

2. When Saturn is in Libra and Jupiter in Cancer, great changes and alterations shall happen in the world.

3. For discovering such grand mutations we should well consider the great, mean, and lesser conjunctions of the Planets in the several Trigona, the removes of the Superiors from one sign to another, as also their application to the Fixed Stars.

4. Likewise the changes of the Absides[1] of the Planets cause mutations in governments and laws, which is a point very much to be regarded.

5. Mercury with an unfortunate Planet in the eleventh denotes the establishment of some severe or unjust laws in the world.

6. A Conjunction of Mars and Saturn in the sixth or eighth house, especially in a humane sign, signifies a great Pestilence.

7. When in the Radix of any City Mars shall be in the

---

[1] A very old term used to denote the points of situation termed Apogee and Perigee.

Mid-heaven, the inhabitants will be inclined to Sedition. If Saturn be there they will be very mischievous, yet very laborious.

8. If Wars be signified, note the Angle of the figure wherein Mars is posited, for from that Part the Enemies shall come.

End of the Aphorisms of Cardan

Fifty of the Principal Fixed Stars

Showing their true Longitude, Latitude, Magnitude, and Natures, to the Year of Christ 1700, January 1. For every Year before, subtract, and every Year after add 50 seconds to or from their Longitude in the Table, and you have their true places for any time past, present, or to come.

Star	Long.	Lat.	Mag.	Nature
The Star in the end of the Wing of Pegasus	5♈00	12N35	2	♂ ☿
The Head of Andromeda	10♈09	25N42	2	♃ ♀
Whale's Belly	13♈47	25S01	4	♄
The Girdle of Andromeda	26♈11	25N59	2	♀
Southern Star in the former Horn of the Ram	29♈59	7N08	4	♄ ♂
The following Horn of the Ram	29♈45	8N29	4	♄ ♂
Bright Star in the Head of the Ram	3♉28	9N57	3	♂ ♄
The Left Foot of Andromeda	10♉01	27N46	2	♀

Star	Long.	Lat.	Mag.	Nature
The Bright Star in the Jaw of the Whale	10♉19	12S37	2	♄
The Head of Medusa	21♉59	22N22	3	♄ ♃
The middle and bright Star of the Seven Stars	25♉46	1N00	3	♂ ☽
The North Eye of the Bull	4♊15	2S36	3	♀
The South Eye called Aldebaran, Patilicium	5♊34	5S31	2	♂
The Bright Foot of Orion, Rigel	12♊49	31S11	1	♃ ♄
The former Shoulder of Orion	16♊45	16S53	2	♂ ☿
The Shee-Goat	17♊48	22N51	1	☿ ♂
The former Star in Orion's Belt	18♊12	23S38	2	♃ ♄
The middle Star in Orion's Belt	19♊16	24S33	2	♃ ♄
The highest Star in the Head of Orion	19♊33	13S26	4	♃ ♄
The Star in the extremity of the South Horn of the Bull	20♊34	2S14	3	♂

Star	Long.	Lat.	Mag.	Nature
The following Shoulder of Orion	24♊34	16S06	2	♂ ☿
Propus	26♊44	0S13	4	♂
The right Shoulder of Auriga	27♊14	21N27	2	♂ ☿
The bright Foot of Gemini	4♋53	6S48	2	☿ ♀
Higher Head of Castor, Apollo	16♋00	10N02	2	♂ ♀ ♄
Pollux, Hercules	19♋05	6N38	2	♂
The Lesser Dog	21♋40	15S57	2	☿ ♂
Praesepe	3♌28	1N14	Neb	♂ ☽
The North Assellus	3♌19	3N08	4	♂ ☉
The South Assellus	4♌30	0S04	4	♂ ☉
The Heart of Hydra	23♌05	22S24	1	♄ ♀
Basiliscus, Cor Leonis, Regulus	25♌20	0N26	1	♂
The middle Star in the Lyon's Neck	25♌22	8N47	1	♄ ☿
The back of the Lyon	7♍03	14N20	2	♄ ♀
The tail of the Lyon	17♍25	12N18	1	♄ ♀ ☿
Vindemiatrix	5♍45	16N15	3	♄ ♀ ☿
The Star under the Virgin's Girdle	7♍17	8N41	3	☿ ♀

Star	Long.	Lat.	Mag.	Nature
The Virgin's Spiek, Arista	19♎38	1N59	1	♀♂
South Ballance	10♏53	0N25	2	♄♀
North Ballance	15♏10	8N35	2	♃♂
Left Hand of Ophiucus	2♏08	17N19	3	♂♄
Higher Star in the Forehead of the Scorpion	28♏58	1N05	2	♄♀
The left knee of Ophiucus	5♐02	11N30	3	♂♃
The Scorpion's Heart, Antares	5♐35	4S27	1	☿♂♃
The right knee of Ophiucus	13♐48	7N18	3	♄♀
Bright Star in the hand of the Water Bearer	27♑31	8N10	4	♀☿
Bright Star of the Vulture	27♑31	29N21	2	♄☿
The Mouth of Pegasus	7♒24	22N07	3	☿♀
Fomalhaut	29♒33	21S00	1	♀☿
Marchab Pegasi	19♒18	19N26	2	♂☿
South Tail of the Whale	29♓18	20S47	2	♄

www.ingramcontent.com/pod-product-compliance
Lightning Source LLC
Chambersburg PA
CBHW032102080426
42733CB00006B/380